The ~~Seven~~

A Practical Occult Experience

By Francois Lepine

F.Lepine Publishing

Copyright 2004

ISBN: 978-0-9781105-3-6

www.Nagah.org

Table of contents

Introduction

Seven virtues and seven vices; fourteen strings pulling the morality of our human ego. We are not empty, but filled with thoughts, currents and memories, and we are always subject to the outside manifestations of what resides inside of us. We may develop great power, but we can achieve our goals only by becoming responsible of this inner power. To master our animal reactions and to develop virtuous behaviors, this is the only way to attain full realization of our potential, and ultimately find peace.

« The Seven Seals » is a metaphor of the occult tools we can aspire to develop, as a human, but also as a spiritual being. By observing nature, specifically the human nature, we have become masters at understanding how we work inside our minds, but also have we become adepts at hiding ourselves from the truth. Above power, there is truth. Engulfed in this truth we cease to be simple human animals; we become filled with the essence that composes the whole of the universe, and we finally understand everything. Many paths are pointing to the heavens, but all of them are challenging, either at the mental or the emotional level, some even at the physical level.

In this book, we wish to guide you through a new occult experience. The material is presented in a specific order that should awaken you to new spiritual concepts. Once you have gone through the entire book, it will still be useful as a reference on occult correspondences. We will review a few aspects of the occidental occult sciences, from different traditions, but mostly revolving around the concept of the seven seals. We will continue by revealing ancient methods used by the Masters of these arts, methods that usually were reserved only for the most devoted disciples. We wish to share this science with you in order to possibly awaken some knowledge that you might already hold, buried deep inside your consciousness. Many of you have abilities that have yet to be discovered, while others simply need guidance to direct their experience with more efficiency.

Our first goal is to open a door, for you to consider passing through. You will be encouraged to become your own master, not to be influenced by outside sources or dogmas. It is important to give credit to the competent teachers. It does not mean that you have to give up your own personal integrity to do so. By learning to trust yourself, you will be able to trust others, and maybe will you open your mind to higher sources of knowledge; but do not forget who you are and who is in charge of your life: yourself.

There is a challenge that all spiritual seekers have to face: we exist and function with our human ego. All that was depicted as sin: jealousy, gluttony, avarice… all that continuously results in deceit and confrontation, all of these are the basic attitudes of our human ego. It was once necessary to be possessive of our territory, of our mates, or to envy the neighbor's clan, to ensure our survival. Although useful at the time, these animal traits are not necessary anymore. Do not judge yourself too hard; these behaviors made it possible for human kind to exist this far. Nonetheless, it is only by mastering ourselves that we may attain truth and peace.

In this book, you will go thru many different types of exercises and techniques, even complete rituals. There will also be introspection methods, encouraging you to look inward to find yourself. If you read chapter by chapter, and do the techniques one after the other in the order they are exposed to you, you might just become more aware of your higher spiritual reality, following the ways that have been done for thousands of years by the spiritualists of the occident.

To expose the seven seals in their most sacred approach, we have also provided an important ancient text of theurgia called the "Arbatel of Magick", written around 1575. It is written in old English but is quite easy to follow. It will inspire you in the ways that the ancient mages practiced this wonderful art of communion with the universal forces. Then, the book is concluded with the art of elemental magic, encouraging you to develop harmonious relationships with the spiritual world that populates our beautiful nature.

Reserved in the seven occult seals are vast banks of spiritual knowledge, and a promise of freedom. Seven virtues to develop, seven sins to conquer, associated with accessible practices and rituals that will produce tangible results as you progress on your own spiritual path. We will encourage you to discover your own ways and to use the tools you prefer. Whatever the path you chose, the truth remains the same, and with Faith, you might just become a Master of the Seven Seals.

Theory Overview

Here we direct you to the basic theory behind our practices and rituals, in many fields of knowledge and traditions. It is impossible to give all the information about each of these traditions, so immense their knowledge bases are, it would take a thousand lifetimes to put everything in here. We encourage you to learn more about a subject if you feel attracted to it; it will enhance your life as well as your spiritual experience. This book will accentuate itself on the practical aspects of occidental occult sciences.

Planes of existence

The human experience is lived on many levels simultaneously. Here is only a brief description of the different planes of human existence. More information will be found in latter chapters. Most people are only aware of the physical reality. Even then, it is filtered with the conditionings of the mind. A few people will also be aware of their mental activity. For the emotional plane, the candidates are even harder to find. Very few people feel the plane of willpower and bioelectricity.

The four planes of the human existence are as follow:

1- Mental

2- Emotional

3- Ethereal

4- Physical

Note that there are other planes of existence at the spiritual level, but right now, the goal of our practice is to become a master of our human dimensions.

The mental plane is the plane where we think. Many people think, but very few are "aware" of the mental activity and it's different processes. To become aware of the activity of your mental dimension, you have to study yourself meticulously. There is a necessity to discover which mental patterns you perpetuate because of social conditioning. These conditioning patterns help us integrate ourselves in society, but when we are not aware of them, they prevent us from reaching mental freedom. We must not get rid of our conditionings, but we must refine them so that they can serve our expansion rather than fix us into present behaviors without awareness. The mental plane is where the conscious learning process begins.

In the emotional plane reside desire, fear and anger. It is the plane of attraction and repulsion (although every plane has its polarity mechanism). It is the plane where we define our preferences, most of the time out of reflexes coming from buried fear or anger. Even people who think they are confident will show subtle signs of darker emotions behind their choices and behaviors. It is easy to make a mask of confidence and self-trust, but beneath we often fight between our desires, our fears and our angers. To be aware of the emotional plane, we must accept to feel pain inside, from time to time, but we should not play the role of the victim and sink into depression. Let yourself feel your emotions without playing a game of victim, persecutor, or savior. Pay attention to your decisions, and be aware of what motivates your choices. One motive is not always better than another. The goal here is to be aware and accept to feel emotions, not to judge their pertinence with senseless intellectualism.

The ethereal plane is the place of willpower, determination, activity and energy. This plane is the container of our bioelectricity, our life-force. It is the level where resides the oriental Chi. This plane can be weak with laziness, or strong with activity. In order for the spiritual energies from the higher planes to get down to the physical plane, the ethereal energy body must be active, and its channels must be kept clean. Do breathing exercises and physical exercises to keep your energy body healthy. To become aware of this energy body, you have to pay attention to the little feelings of flowing energy inside your limbs. Many people could feel those energy flows, but are so mentally unavailable to be aware of themselves that they can't even accept that such a thing is possible.

The physical plane is the finality of creation, and it is also the place where we naturally learn, since it is the plane where our senses are naturally active. In the physical world, everything takes place. This is the plane to be aware of, to pay attention to, because here are manifested all the signs, lessons and dreams of our Spirit. We will give more chance to our evolution by keeping a good physical health. Yet, it is not necessary to become an athlete. In the physical plane will be projected every situation found on other planes of existence. You should take the time to observe your physical body and your physical surroundings, to find out what you could resolve or make better in your life. Every problem you will rectify in the physical plane with awareness will also be rectified in the other planes of existence.

Develop virtues in your heart and your mind; act with power and gentleness; move and rectify your physical experience; and the spiritual worlds will open up to you, revealing their powers and abilities for you to use. The first results will come quickly. Then, you might even be tempted to use these new tools without virtue, and that might just let you manifest more lessons in life. Isn't it great to receive from life what you put into it!

Kabalah

Kabalah is the origin of most occidental occult sciences and magical systems. It has been used by all the mages and wise men for thousands of years. In this science, the human being is considered to be a universe in itself. First developed by the Jewish people, followed by the Christian occultists, this profound concept of the workings of the universe is applied to the Macro-cosmos, the big universe, and the Micro-cosmos, the small universe of the human being. Although anyone's interpretation is personal to each his own path, we will notice that we get a more authentic experience by respecting the original Hebrew texts. In fact, the only way to get to the core of Kabalah is to read the original Hebrew text like a kabalist would, with the understanding of the tradition. Nonetheless, It is useful to start with the simple and mentally accessible tools that Kabalah provides.

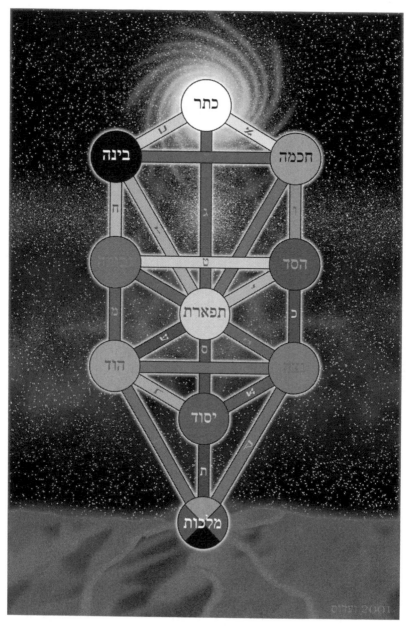

Kabbalistic Tree of Life

The Tree of Life is a graphical representation of the complete system of Kabalah. It represents 10 planes of existence linked together by 22 types of energies that exist in the universe. Each of the 10 planes of existence is a sphere called "Sephirot" and it contains all the experience and creative power of this specific plane. These 22 links between them took form in the shape of the 22 letters of the Hebrew alphabet. These 22 letters of the Hebrew alphabet gave birth to the 22 major cards of the tarot, to astrological signs, to the name of angels,... almost every occult science of the occident has a link to Kabalah.

Kabalah is a very rich science that explains every aspect of human existence in an intellectually understandable way. Beware, this science is deep and mysterious, and it could lead you to break your mind if you are too much in a hurry. Learning must be accompanied with prayer and meditation. The more you understand the principles of Kabalah, the more your practices will become efficient. It is not necessary to learn Hebrew in order to become a good occultist, but it will help if you at least learn the basics of the language, like the Hebrew alphabet.

The Pentagram from Eliphas Levi is a good example of applied occult symbolism derived from Kabalah. Every detail has its own importance and adds to the efficiency of the talisman. The true power comes from understanding the meaning of the symbols that create the final design. It is an inspiration for virtue and wisdom. It renders its full efficiency when the occultist has developed inside himself, the virtues that the symbols represent. Although the traditional Jewish Kabalists will not endorse this modern version of the pentagram, it has been an important part of the learning process for new modern Kabalah students.

The best way to learn the occult mysteries is to practice daily, to do the rituals, and to meditate on the symbols. Meditate also on the lessons of life. It is with your heart that you become an occultist, not with your mind. The goal of the theory is to fill your mind with knowledge enough to connect you with other higher realities of understanding, and by then, all the knowledge of the world will not replace the bliss of simply being in contact with the truth.

The tree of life

The Kabalah theory is based on this diagram, both marvelous and complex. It was first explained in a book called "Sepher Yetzirah", the book of formation. It is a manual on universal mechanics. It explains how the light of creation condensed itself to create the many aspects of the universe and the human being. The Kabalists say "As above, so below, as below, so above". It's their way of saying we were made the same way the universe was made.

The great light of creation came from the "Absolute light without end", and poured down like water to fill in ten spheres of existence, like jars. The water of creation filled the first, then overflowed into the second, then overflowed into the third, down to the tenth jar/sphere. These jars/spheres are called "sephirot".

The channels used by the flowing light of creation link the sephiroth together and so permit the flow from one sphere to another. There are 22 of these channels, each represented by a letter of the Hebrew alphabet.

In each sephirot, God takes a shape, one of his infinite manifestations. Each sephirot has a universal soul, an envelope of itself. In each sephirot, a "manager" resides, to lead its operations, and this manager is called an archangel. In each sephirot also live concepts and spiritual beings, and lastly, each sephirot takes on a physical shape, a body, a planetary shape. Therefore, each sephirot has 5 distinct components: 1- God form, 2- Soul, 3- Regent/manager, 4- Family of spiritual beings, 5- Physical manifestation.

By learning about each aspect of these sephirot, and the 22 links between them, we can invoke the spiritual energy of the universal mechanics to help us in our lives, assist our development and resolve some problems. From this theory came all forms of occidental magic, divination, astrology, numerology, tarot, and so on. The 22 major cards of the tarot are in fact the 22 channels of Kabalah's Tree of Life. We do not recommend big long rituals with enormous amounts of details and artifacts; at least, not at first. You may learn about these complex forms of rituals if you learn practical Kabalah on your own, which is good. Many books are available in good libraries.

Here is the basic diagram called the « Tree of life », with its 10 sephiroth numbered in order of their creation. They all have names in Hebrew that will be given later. With patience, you can learn to understand its basic principles and start working with it. Start by understanding the direct meaning of each God name, sphere, regent, entities, planet… to invoke them in your prayers.

(Sephiroth is already the plural word for Sephirah, a single of these spheres, thus we do not pluralize the word Sephiroth in English.)

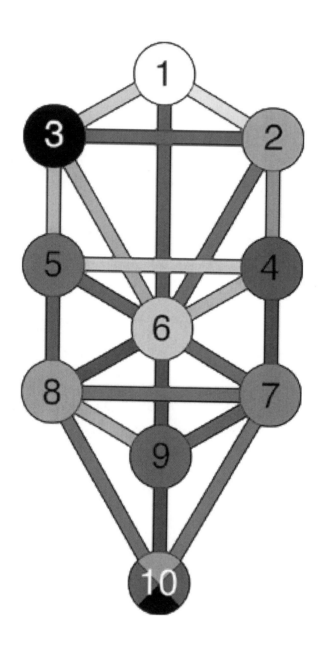

The pentagram

The pentagram is a five (penta) point image (gram) made out of one continuous line with five equal angles. It calls upon the force of the fifth sephirah named Geburah, the strength, and the concept of movement and action. Therefore, it is used in rituals to initiate the action of the operation, to call for a movement of energy.

It is represented in your hand, with five fingers, but most of all, it is represented in your body, with your five extremities: 2 legs, 2 arms and your head. The pentagram with one point pointing up and two pointing down is the symbol of the virtuous man. Using this symbol will encourage you to act with virtue, and expand the implication of your consciousness in your actions.

The pentagram can also be reversed to symbolize the falling man, or the decadent being. It has two points pointing up, and only one pointing down. It is mostly used by unconscious and uninformed black mages, and does not really promote expansion of consciousness.

Depending on the direction of the pentagram's energy flow, it is either summoning of banishing, inviting or pushing away. In the Lower Earth Banishing Pentagram Ritual, we are starting from the earth point, lower left, and doing a clockwise movement, to the upper point, then the lower right, left point, then the right point, and finishing at the beginning, at the lower left. This is somewhat a clockwise movement and it banishes. It starts at the earth point, so it banishes lower dense energies. Deamons (lower spirits) and ghosts are usually afraid of this banishing pentagram.

In rituals, you will be asked to draw the pentagram in mid air, with your fingers. Some importance will be given to the elements associated with each point. The following figure shows the position of each element on the rectified pentagram. You can understand that the reversed pentagram has the spirit below the four elements, implicating that the human animal would be stronger than the spiritual being.

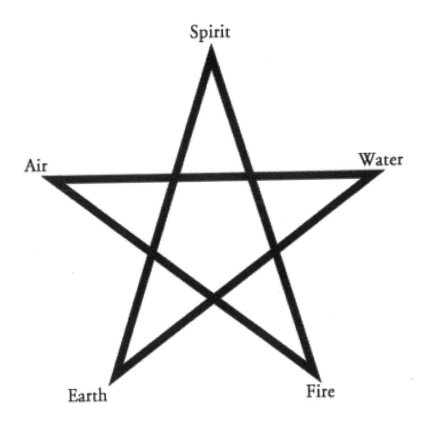

When you invoke the pentagram in your rituals, you must see it clearly in your mind and put some energy in believing it is really there. The pentagram has to vibrate in the spiritual planes with your willpower, and with determinate visualization. It must also vibrate with the energy of its purpose, with the goal of your ritual.

When used in a ritual, it is not only a physical drawing, but an astral tool to create energy movements. Be careful in your experiments with the pentagram. Learn the basics with the Lesser Earth Banishing Pentagram Ritual, further in the ritual section of this book.

The more you understand the meaning of the kabalistic words in these rituals, the more powerful will be the effects. The more virtuous you become, the more efficient and quick theses rituals will work. Develop yourself with study, virtue and faith.

Life is the name of God vibrating

God, the absolute highest form of God, is undefined, without name and shape. It can't be known, understood or spoken. It can't be described, since it does not exist in a manifested form, at no level of the created universe. Yet, it is everything manifested, since all is a part of the Absolute God. It is the creator, it is absolute un-created void and it is also all things, both null and complete. The mind can't grasp the concept; it can only accept that there is a concept, and that only faith can grasp it.

The names of God are the highest masks over the face of the absolute, undefined God. Calling the names of God, we tap into the highest form of energy available to humans. The absolute God flows thru his creation, and thru the masks he holds over his creation, so we can see one side of him, one at a time. By calling a name of God, we are summoning his most holy power to flow thru us, and permitting him to change us.

Beware, the power of God is strong, and some might even feel sick and unstable after a serious call to God. Go softly, only for a few minutes at a time. When you feel ready, summon one name of God for 20 minutes, then meditate peacefully, trying to listen to the silent words of God, thru this thin veil between you and the absolute infinite. In time, you will be able to chant one single name of God for an hour, and feel its power flow thru you.

The first power you should acquire is the power of discerning, the power to choose, without judging, but with great care of the good and evil implicated in each of your choices. This can be summoned by the name of the Lord of the Earth World "Adonaï Ha-Aretz", or the name of the Lord of the kingdom "Adonaï Melek". This produces free will, and frees you.

Then, the power to live and be productive from the Almighty God of Life "Shadaï El-Haï".

Knowledge, balance, manifestation, the name of the Gods of Armies "Elohim Tzebaoth".

Creativity, sensuality, love, feeling, from the Lord of Armies "Yehovah Tsebaoth".

Wisdom, kingship, respect, advancement, from the God of Wisdom "Eloha Ve-Daath".

Power, martial, military, force, from the Gods Strong "Elhoim Gibor".

Peace, misericord, compassion, leadership, from God Consciousness "EL".

The highest, the law, funeral, life and death, immortality, from God Creator "Yehovah".

Movement of the universe, the mobile behind the creation, from "Iah".

Sit before God, the original, and dive into infinite, from "Eheïeh".

Before you chant any of these names of God, learn about the tree of life, the kabalistic science of the formation of the universe. Chant the song of the tree of life (see Rituals), and start slowly. If you go too fast, your life will be affected by the power of change, justice, the purgatory and its fire burning your impurities faster than usual. Learn, develop virtues, and practice breathing the life force of God, and you will prepare your body and mind to receive the names of God into your body and mind.

The Light is everywhere

For the mystic, the Light is the force within the elements. It is the power moving beyond the atoms, and binding atoms together to form matter, physical and spiritual planes, life forms as well as inanimate objects.

« The Light is everywhere, the Light is everything. »

Contemplation of this thought will make your human mind available to feel the force beyond matter. It will be essence of life beyond fire, the creative organic laws beyond water, the harmony of movement beyond air, the strength and stability beyond earth. Beyond the particles that form physical matter, there is energy.

This energy came from God, and God gave it a shape. This is the act of creation. The constructing and moving of matter, the assembling and changing of matter, this is the Light, the Heavenly and earthly forces working within the composition of the elements that form all that there is.

The Light is a symbol only for the mind, it is an inspiration for the heart, a potential for the will, and truth for the spirit. There is a truth higher than the Light, which is the truth of Being. Do not believe that the Light is the highest, because the highest is God. The Light is the work of God in the process. Contemplate the Light to let your human self and bodies accept its work within you and around you. Contemplate the Light to enhance yourself, to know that you are beyond the Light as a spiritual being, and that the Light is available to you as a human. You must respect the Light, the Tool of God.

Understanding the basic theories of quantum physics will help you understand the Light. Meditating on the Light will let you know its essence, and yourself. The Light is everywhere, the Light is Everything.

Practices

As you start doing these practices, we encourage you to eat well and do some physical exercise, to keep your body in good health. Some practices are more demanding than others. Respect your limits, while always trying to go beyond them safely. Since some of these practices might raise your body temperature aggressively, we encourage you to drink a lot of water and be aware of the emotions that rise in you.

It is good to experiment with all of the techniques at least once, so you will know which ones you prefer. Then, give more time to the practices you prefer. Follow your heart and do not doubt yourself. The first subtle results will come quickly; then a longer period of time might pass before you see any tangible results, while your energy level rises. Do not do these practices only for their results, but also for what they provide immediately, while you are doing them. Before anything, seek Love and understanding, then the power will come all by itself. If you seek power, it will take much more time for the effects to manifest, and they will not be as impressive.

Of the body

Breathing

In every occult practice, conscious breathing is very important. It is the base physical action that supports the flow of energy into your body, and it will help spiritual light flow thru your spiritual bodies. We will also explain a simple technique, inspired by the Chinese people, used to gather light inside your body, storing energy in your abdomen.

Normal and reversed breathing

Normal breathing :

A normal breath is very different than the automatic breathing cycles that keep you alive when you are not thinking about breathing. The reason is simple; no one really breathes correctly when they are not thinking about it. Some people take in only 11 ml of oxygen per minute, way far from the minimum oxygen your body needs to be healthy. A normal breath is a healthy breath.

The inhalation should fill your lungs almost completely without straining your abdomen or diaphragm. The breath should naturally fill your abdomen, without raising your upper torso. A deep breath should not even make your higher ribs move. Place your hand over your heart, where your ribs connect to the sternum, between your solar plexus and your throat. Take a deep breath and feel if your ribs are moving. If they do, you are filling your upper lungs too much and not enough air is getting to the bottom of your lungs. Although it is impossible to keep your rib cage immobile (and that is not the goal), it should move as little as possible without requiring effort.

When you exhale, let your abdomen rest until the air doesn't come out naturally anymore, and pull your abdomen in lightly without force. It won't completely empty your lungs. If your ribs are moving inward or downward too much, it means you lifted them upward while you inhaled, or that you filled the upper part of your lungs too much.

Breath in
Abdomen out
Upper chest normal

Breath out
Abdomen normal
Upper chest normal

When you breathe normally, it is your abdomen that pushes out slightly and pulls in slightly, as you inhale and exhale. The breathing cycle should not require excessive force, but it should fill your lungs up to 80% of your maximum capacity. To fill your lungs to 100% of its capacity require effort, and it is not natural. When you breathe out with force, pulling in your abdomen lightly at the end of the breath, empties your lungs to 20% or 10% of its capacity. The same for emptying your lungs totally, force is applied more than the natural state.

To experiment, your can try filling your lungs completely (without hurting yourself) and keep your rib cage as immobile as possible, then keep the air in for 10 seconds and breathe out completely, keeping your breath out for 10 seconds. Let all your muscles go and let your body breathe without influencing it and look at the difference. Now, do a normal breath, filling your lungs down to your abdomen with at least a little effort, but lightly. Keep the air in 3 seconds and let it out without any effort, but a light pulling inward of your abdomen at the end of exhalation.

This is what we mean by "normal breath". It will be used in practices that focus on the elevation of self, meditation, mental and spiritual training, while the reversed breath is used in physical development, opening the channels of energy in your body, enhancing your ability to manifest your energy on the physical plane.

Reversed breathing

To clearly understand the principle of reversed breathing, you must first practice accurate normal breathing. This is important to keep your rib cage almost motionless while doing the reversed breathing. The reversed breathing cycle is used to concentrate the energy, in a way that will make it denser, compacting it so it can become available on the physical plane.

As an example, forget about the normal breathing method and let the instinctive breath come along. Imagine yourself in a situation of alert, of defending yourself, of being ready for action, and while closing your fists, take in a quick deep breath without thinking. Most of you will notice that the abdomen pulled in while you were breathing in, and it pushes out lightly when you exhale. Experiment a bit.

When in danger, the body automatically does a reversed breath, getting ready to put energy in a physical action. The quick part was only for the example. The reversed breath method goes as smoothly as the normal breath unless stated otherwise.

Breath in

Abdomen pulled in

Upper chest normal

Breath out

Abdomen let out

Upper chest normal

When we are working with methods that focus on manifesting physical phenomena, we will be doing reversed breathing. The upper rib cage still doesn't move, and you should breathe slowly and comfortably. As you breathe in, contract your abdomen pulling it in lightly. As you breathe, let go of your abdominal muscles completely, pushing out lightly at the end of the exhalation, without force.

Gathering energy method

Before you do anything with energy, you must have energy reserves to work with. With no energy in reserve, you will deplete your own life force. I hope you understand that this is NOT GOOD! Gathering energy is quite simple, and you can practice about anywhere you don't need to concentrate. Don't do this while driving, or even while you are a passenger. When you gather energy, you and everyone around you will get a little bit more prone to lose their concentration. Everyone could get sleepy, or hyper, or feel weird sensations in their body, especially if they are not used to feeling energy.

Storing energy in your abdomen

Place you palms on your abdomen, just below your navel (fig. 1). You should have your left palm inside, touching your abdomen, and the right palm over the left. If you are standing, bend the knees a bit. If you are sitting, try to keep your spine up straight, and do not cross your legs while you do this method.

While you inhale, visualize white light coming from all around you, penetrating all the pores of your skin, fill your body and go into your inner abdomen. While you exhale, all this white energy is condensed into a concentrated ball of light in your inner abdomen, in the middle of your body just below the level of your navel. Gather energy by breathing normally, deeply, and calmly. Take in energy from all around you and concentrate it in your inner abdomen.

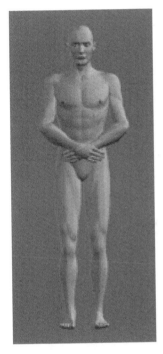

Fig.1

Standing up, do a few normal breathing and relax. Bend your knees slightly and start.

As you breathe in, imagine white light come from above your head, and enter thru your head like white wind, going in a continuous flow to your lower abdomen (fig. 2). As you breathe out, the energy stays in your lower abdomen and becomes a ball of light. Do 9 relaxed breaths absorbing from the head. It is a normal reflex to tighten the muscles of the abdomen and the arms when you do this for the first time. Try doing it with will, while keeping your muscles relaxed.

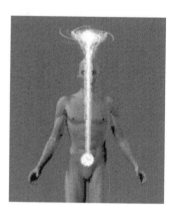

Fig. 2

Do the same with the arms. Extend your arms to the sides, placing your palms facing away from you, and inhale energy thru the middle of your two palms, leading it down to your lower abdomen. Do it 9 times and try to keep your body relaxed.

Then with the feet, taking the wind like energy thru the middle of your two feet, leading it to your lower abdomen, strengthening the white energy ball.

Once you did 9 breaths of each, filling your abdomen from the head, from the hands and the feet, do all three at the same time, totaling 5 entry points for the energy, filling your lower abdomen with 9 energy breaths. (fig. 3)

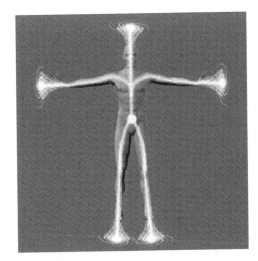

Fig.3

Finish by placing your palms over your abdomen and doing a few normal breaths. This will help to store the energy you gathered.

Of the heart

The truth about yourself

Recognising the truth

Truth, honesty, integrity. To recognize the truth, you must first understand it. And as we will explain it, you'll understand that it is hard to grasp. Truth refers to a state of mind, while honesty refers to the communication of facts. Integrity refers to respect of self.

Truth, the philosophical truth, is beyond the physical reality of facts. It is the absolute expression of what IS, both at a spiritual and human level. It is a place without doubt, without darkness, where there is no communication between two parties. It rather is a completeness, a communion. Recognizing the truth has nothing to do with affirming actual facts, confirming physical events. It is the recognition that we are "all", that we are everything, that we ARE.

Down to earth, recognizing the truth means that we accept every possible aspect of the human existence as a part of us, as a possibility, and not necessarily as an actual fact. You must not judge what is Truth. If you can say to yourself "I am a liar, I am egocentric", then you are in truth. It does not mean that you lied, right now, about a particular subject, but that you recognize the truth. If you lied only once in your lifetime, you are a liar. You must also be able to accept that you are honest, since you told the truth at least once in your lifetime. If you lacked charity and goodness at least once in your lifetime, you are egocentric. Of course, you are also charitable and kind if you helped out someone for free at least once. Without actually hurting anyone, can you recognize that "I am a killer". Again, do not judge truth. Truth is everything. You might have killed a living creature in your life.

If someone ask you if you just told the truth, don't answer "I am a liar" if you did not lie. Truth has nothing to do with what others perceive of you. In truth, we both know that you are a liar, and it only concerns your personal open mindedness towards your own acceptance of self as a whole. In the same line of thought, we also know you are honest. To answer someone with honesty or not, if you told the truth or lied, concerns your integrity and does not mean you should tell the truth, but rather respect yourself. Usually, telling the truth is encouraged.

With each truth follows a manifestation in each plane of existence. A truth brings up a thought; a truth brings up an emotion. It might motivate action, but we will look at the emotional aspect for now. With a calm deep breath, remember that you are a thief, and feel what emotion it awakens. Recall from your past events where you stole things, time or space. Take your time to think about it, and feel the emotion rising up. Don't go playing a victim game here because this kind of practice will inevitably bring up emotions of guilt. However, don't think you are invulnerable to stealing. Recognize the truth and feel what you are. Accept the emotions linked to your Truth.

Once you felt, once you are aware and conscious, forgive yourself and admit that you are a thief. There is a space that will liberate within you when the guilt smoothly dissolves, while you breathe softly. After taking a few minutes to elevate the emotion, fill this space with joy and compassion, the fruit of forgiveness. This will not change that you are a thief, but it will fill the hole where guilt took place before. You are what you are, recognize the truth.

If you react strongly towards this practice, then you need to develop humility and open your mind. Smoothen your heart and accept all that you can possibly be. Expand the limits of your perception of self. The stronger you react to a truth about yourself, the deeper you are in bullshitting yourself away from truth. You cannot be complete while you flee emotions deep within yourself. You cannot go further without accepting the truth that you are everything.

After you finish one step of the process, take time to remember that you are honest, kind, charitable, happy, young, relaxed, joyful. If you find it difficult to accept your positive truth after this exercise, you are playing a game of "victim" (O, poor you). Be humble and accept your virtuous beauty, without transforming this acceptance into vanity.

Do the same with lying, being arrogant, hypocrite, aggressive, pretentious, egocentric,...

1- Think about a truth
2- Call back some clear memories or impressions from the past
3- Feel the emotion, breathe the emotion
4- Forgive yourself with compassion
5- Uplift yourself with your beautiful truth

Repeat this experience often, so that you will deepen your sensitivity to perceiving the truth, rather than perceiving the simple facts of coincidental events of life. With time, you will not perceive good and evil, beauty and ugliness, but simple consecutive experiences of life. Be happy simply because you live.

You are not great because of what you did, or bad because of what you did. You are great simply because you live.

The goal is to be conscious. Be aware, focused, honest with yourself, and recognize the truth. Forgive yourself your mistakes, since you are here to experiment. You can be sorry for a while, then, you have to take command of your emotional life and be happy, while still being aware of the depths of your human experience.

Taking the rage out

As you practice spiritual techniques, you might become more sensitive to anger at the beginning. When you need to get anger and rage out of your system, forget about meditation and relaxation for a while, there is a volcano burning, your energy structures are stimulated and your system is under the pressure of the change.

Shouting something like "Wrraaaaa!" will help you relieve the pressure. Shout loudly and hit hardly and strongly on a soft surface with your palms, hand opened, fingers stretched out or making a fist. The soft surface can be your bed, the grass, a battle matt. Shout it out, hit hard and contract your lower abdomen muscles when you shout the syllable. Breathe in slowly while releasing your lower abdomen, and give another shot.

At first, it might be artificial but as you go on, after a few times, the rage will encompass you madly and you must simply focus on hitting with your palm or fist on a soft surface and shouting. You might start to cry or react very emotionally. This is good, but do not injure yourself or someone else, or you will step back in the path of mastering this power. Remember where the pain came from, when you felt alone amongst the humans, and forcefully, yet responsibly, get it out of your system.

After a few minutes, sit and look upwards, breathing smoothly. Accept your life. You are the only one that can provide for your needs, but remember that you are not alone. If you hurt yourself or someone else, or break something, you are not practicing self-mastery. Yet, don't wait to be a master before you start practicing as an apprentice, or else you will never master yourself.

Relax, but do not meditate after this practice. Take care of your emotions. Develop compassion and forgiveness. Be soft with yourself for a while. Seek out a silent environment if you can.

Observing the volcano

Anger plays a big part in our reactions towards other people, our environment, and our own life. As we awaken the energies of power within our body, and as we unveil the hidden abilities of our subconscious mind, we will be more tempted to become angry. Therefore, it is important to understand anger and to master it. Master your anger and you will be able develop yourself quicker.

The emotion/energy of anger is exactly the same as joy. It comes from the same source and goes in the same direction, but it simply is not of the same emotional polarity. Anger and joy come from the perineum, at the base of the spine, and it rises into our body to produce an exterior reaction. As you gain self-confidence, you will be more and more tempted to express your joy outwards, as well as your anger. It is important to develop self-confidence, and it is also important to be aware of the consequences and to master the way it is expressed. Trust yourself, and remain aware of yourself.

Anger is a fire that rises into your body, to give you the moral and physical power to defend yourself in case of attack. In the polarity of Joy, it is a power that can feed your energy bodies to manifest into exterior effects. It will give you more strength, more speed, and faster reactions. It will enhance your occult practices. Anger will most likely overwhelm you and bring upon yourself your own defeat, causing you more pain.

Although it comes with pain from inside, anger is not to be let loose; it must be mastered. Look at anger like a spring of lava coming from the earth. It erupts like a volcano, and it takes great courage to sit beside it and relax. But this is exactly what you should do. Even if you are standing up, within yourself, sit on the ground, right beside the lava river and contemplate it. Breathe deeply.

Contract your abdomen and relax it. Give further attention to the moment your abdominal muscles release themselves in the relaxation part. Notice how your body does it. The same way you can relax your abdominal muscles, you will now relax your anger. It will still be there, it will still be painful, but it will stop being active. Relax your "anger muscle". Relax the tension within you. Do not try to become comfortable, because in this moment, you can't be comfortable. Just relax, sit by the lava river, and contemplate the anger volcano erupting, without doing anything. Breathe deeply and calmly. On the outside, make like if nothing was happening, in the inside, know that it is happening and contemplate it.

By mastering this technique, you will be able to master the anger within, and the power will be able to rise within you even more. It will push some more anger and joy. Express your joy aloud, any way you wish, with respect for others. But you know what to do with anger. Calmly, peacefully relax it.

Some people try to do this technique, but the only thing they do is build up more and more anger within them, refraining its expression and causing themselves damage on the physical and nervous level. If you feel a buildup inside you, you are not relaxing the anger, but only containing it. You should let it out without hurting anyone including yourself, without breaking anything. Do not keep it inside. You will know when you are successfully contemplating the volcano. There won't be any more pressure inside, even if their will be conflict and pain, and you will feel the energy available from anger without the destructive aspect attached to it.

The virtues of compassion and humility will help you master the technique, and you will be able to raise your power level even more. If you fail just once in this technique, you cannot pretend to be a master, since you cannot even master yourself. Do not discourage yourself, all masters were not born with complete control of their emotions. The real war comes from within, the real power comes from within, and the real Joy comes from within.

Resolving a problem

When facing a challenge in life, our human ego is always tempted to react quickly according to a preset conditioning that promotes conflict and failure. With time and practice, we can develop new reflexes that are virtuous and focused on peaceful resolution and mutual success. Although these positive reactions can register quickly in our mental processes, at first it will take some patient observation of our innate behaviors.

The first step is to learn how to refrain the instant destructive reactions. We call this virtue Temperance. By temporarily stopping the inner impulses that are strongly calling forth from within to destroy all the people associated with the subject of conflict, and by using an equal force to maintain a peaceful attitude, you are also developing willpower, which will be very useful in the development of your own inner power. While deep breathing is recommended, you may also want to develop forgiveness and compassion.

As long as you keep the false thoughts that "I can't forgive him" or "it's his fault, not mine", you are fleeing your inner power. A powerful master is one who can choose to forgive if he wishes to, even the most outrageous offences. This virtue is called Justice and reflects goodness of heart. It does not mean the other had the right to oppress you, but it means that you are powerful enough to be in charge of the situation, and that you have faith that all will be resolved according to the Divine Justice. Faith is also a virtue to develop. Know, deep within, that all will be fine.

There are three roles used by the human ego in a situation of conflict, and they are usually used to attract attention. These are the roles of persecutor, victim, and savior. The persecutor takes pride in its superior but false strength, by oppressing the victim who in turn seeks attention, hoping to attract a savior, in this deceitful dance of the human drama. Without the intervention of Virtue, only suffering will come out as a result.

We recommend you stop playing the role of the victim when a conflict occurs. Do not silently wish for the pity of others. Be strong and assume your responsibility in every situation. Strength is a virtue that will lead you out of any conflict, without anyone getting hurt. Strength is the will to act according to the ways set by Justice. In the same manner, you should stop playing the role of the persecutor and you should not use Strength to oppress others. This would only be the vice of anger and pride. Finally, do not play the role of the savior when acting according to Justice. The role of the savior only serves the human ego, seeking attention and credit for the application of Justice. In most cases, the savior behaviors are not done according to true Justice and serve only the vice of pride.

When facing a conflict, as you master your temper with Temperance, process the situation with intelligence and seek the solution that is right, according to Justice. Be humble enough to let go of your end of the stick. Without kneeling before injustice, make sure that it is not your own envy, avarice or gluttony inciting you to act in any way. Once you have identified the true Justice in a situation, express it and act according to it; but is it always the wisest way to act? Another virtue is Prudence. Do not put yourself in danger even if Justice would incite you to "take back that gun in the hand of that thief!" Do everything you can to live long enough to develop your virtues.

Many times, we would like to confront any and all injustice we see around us, but that would only be pride, as virtue is not intended to make you lose your wife or husband, your job, or even your life. Be grateful for what you have, make sure to protect it, but be humble enough to kneel before the events of life, and think twice before you act, even when you feel you are accompanied by

Justice and Strength. In some cases, should you be developing the virtue of Charity and Faith?

When you see fit to discuss a problem, do it with peace and all parties should give a chance to each other to express their own point of view. If a war is at hand, calculate if the possible casualties are worth the fight. It is rare that Divine Truth will agree to any kind of war, but it will always encourage the application of Justice.

It is recommended to re-read the last chapter if it contains notions new to you. Meditate on virtues, and work at mastering yourself in your daily life.

A doorway to power

Virtues

The most powerful and direct links to power are the development of virtues. Your energy bodies continuously manifest according to the type of person you are. When you develop virtues, your energy system is more powerful than if you were continuously doing rituals and spiritual practices. With virtues developed, it is like if you were in a continuous state of ritual, of meditation, of contemplation of the beauty of the world. With virtues, you are always in a state of power towards the universe, and the universe obeys those who have developed the means to command it.

Although there are many virtues, here is a brief description of seven major virtues that have a direct implication with the seven seals.

Temperance

Do not give in to anger. Do not give in to judgment. Be compassionate. Endure the pressure when it can help others discover Love. Smile and be happy of what life has given you.

Accept your role in the universe, and work to discover it. Do not be susceptible. Do not take anything personally. Be careful of your words when you answer back to some offense. When people offend you, tell them you are sorry if you have offended them.

Justice

Integrity, honesty, truth. Act in ways you know are right. Do your best to respect the human laws of your country. Over that, do what you think is best according to the laws of the universe. It can take some time to understand the laws of the universe, but deep within, all of us know what is right or wrong. Do not make decisions that would lead you to abuse. Do not let yourself be abused by anyone. Accept to earn less when it is right to do so, and defend your right to profit when it is right to do so.

Strength

Move! Do not stop unless it is necessary. Determine yourself to peaceful actions. Make a plan and deploy the necessary energy to accomplish it. Do some physical exercises to enhance your physical strength. Then, transpose the feeling of strength to a higher level, with analogy as a tool. This will help you understand the mystic symbolism of inner strength, of self-empowerment.

Faith

The universe, the great Love of the universe, will take care of you. Know that you are in a classroom, in an experience to learn to master yourself. Realize all of your projects with the assistance of God. Take care of the matters of God, and God will take care of your human matters. God is without shape, without name, without any definite identity. He is the absolute truth of the universe, and he loves you. You are never alone. Thus, all will be fine.

Charity

Give to others without any return. Do not expect recognition or payback. Give without any expectation. Do not ruin yourself. Do not give your physical means of subsistence; It would not be prudent. Give your time, give compassion, take care of others, and take care of yourself in the process. Give love only to give love. Give yourself the opportunity to love others more than you have done yesterday. Take care of your heart in the process, and do not play the "savior" game.

Prudence

Think about it before you move. Develop trust, and develop a sense of responsibility. Make sure of what you are doing. Be careful with any detail. Do not think that nothing will go wrong, take care of it personally. Study, set everything in place, and counter verify. Then act. Do not stop because of fear; hesitation is not prudence.

Hope

A higher version of having a positive attitude, hope is a more tangible expression of faith and self-trust. It is a determination to never give in to negativity, never to play the victim of the events that compose your life. Smile, trust yourself, be positive, and know that all will be fine. It is easy to keep this attitude alive when you know, deep inside, that every event that seems negative is only a lesson to go thru, an experience of knowledge sent by your higher consciousness.

Implication

Many wish to develop great power with little implication, little investment, and little time. It is possible to develop yourself quickly, but self-implication cannot be avoided.

Value and exchange

It is important to see value in the sacred knowledge you acquire. It is important to cherish it and not to throw it freely at anyone who would then destroy or mutilate it. The occult knowledge is too important to be considered invaluable. You must keep it for yourself, and reveal it only when the seeker before you has shown signs of implication and respect. There is a spiritual cost to reveal occult secrets of great value to anyone without respect. When monks wanted to learn something from their master, they had to work hard all day, and bring some food with them. Then, the master would see the balance of the exchange, and he would reveal some esoteric knowledge to the seeker. There must not be abuse in the exchange, but nonetheless, there must be a balanced exchange. You must never ruin yourself to acquire occult knowledge, but you surely will not acquire knowledge of great value without some kind of effort and sacrifice.

You will develop great power only when you affirm within yourself that you value the sacred knowledge, and when you physically act in ways to protect and cherish this knowledge. We call this attitude the "Sense of the sacred". It is a required quality to achieve any great power in any occult field.

Time and willpower

You will not develop a psychic power by doing 5 minutes of a method only once. You will not even attain anything by doing 1 hour, and immediately stop because of the lack of results.

To develop great power, you must practice a minimum of 5 minutes per day, every day of the week, and once a week, do at least one consecutive hour. Do something everyday, even a simple salutation to your altar, but do it.

To develop yourself quickly, you can try with 20 minutes each day, for an entire month. All of those who acted with determination towards their own spiritual path have achieved some transformation and elevation from within. If nothing happens inside, you might not be implicating yourself with a "sacred" attitude, with respect for the value of the knowledge.

Some freaks used techniques for 30 minutes each day of the week, and 1 full hour of practice sometime in the weekend. After only 3 months, they are feeling flows of energy, getting results in their personal life, becoming aware of behavioral patterns which they did not notice before. Upon that, they studied esoteric knowledge, kept a sacred attitude, and took care of their bodies. They became powerful quickly.

Determine yourself and do it. If you take only 5 minutes per day, everyday, you will get results.

Intelligent people can develop quite impressive plans to make the events to occur as they wish, but are these actions done in accordance with the laws of nature, with everyone concerned aware of the orchestration? The reptilian mind is the source of all manipulation. When one does not wish to face an obstacle, he might as well manipulate the events to attain his goals without ever having to face the obstacles. This leads to manipulation, chaos, misunderstanding, fear, pain, and anger. An obstacle is always there to face, or to resolve. Of course, the solution is not always to jump in the face of the obstacle and try to beat it down with hard blows. Violence is also not a solution, either physically or with words.

The reptilian mind will always opt for the camouflage and the illusion. If it sees the opportunity, it will strike to defeat. This behavior is manifested in our human actions and words. It is necessary to stay aware and to act with justice. We do not have the right to ask for justice when we act without it the moments we turn our back. Before we demand respect for our rights, we have to assume our responsibility in front of our higher Spirit, and act accordingly.

Elevating yourself

Imagine yourself a knight, dressed in shiny full plate armor. You have small white feather wings in your back, the human version of the spiritual wings of the angels. You are stepping with your right foot on the head of a snake. Breathe deeply, with gladness and power, for a few minutes.

The snake, the animal, the reptile, is a part of your self. You, as a divine being, are stepping on your own head, as a human reptile. Every human has an arrogant attitude hidden somewhere, that will get out the moment he feels powerful. Develop the ability to be humble while in a situation of power. Power must not be pride. Seek deep within yourself: do you wish to invoke pride and merit with this power? Do you still breathe to the bottom of your abdomen, or did you cut off your abdominal muscles with pride?

Experience 1: Practice yourself at being humble. On a prepared day, do not speak a single word for the entire day. Not even a sound should come out of your mouth. Your vocal cords should not even vibrate. No sign language, no writing, no communication at all, in any way. If you try this experience, you might see that your human animal self wants to control the events and fight with the experience. You should arrange your experience in a way to be alone for the entire day, and be in a very calm environment. Those who wish to do it together would trigger even more inner fighting to speak to the other. This would be good for the experience. Try to remain silent.

Experience 2: Prevent yourself from using or doing something you really like, while at the same time triggering the wish to do/use it. For example, if you like pepper and salt on your food, put the pepper and salt in front of you for the entire meal, without even touching them, but looking at them from time to time. Do this for an entire week with a single item. Practice at depriving yourself of a little something, to be able to endure with more ease when you have to be deprived of something bigger.

These two experiences will help you develop willpower. When you have to face a situation where you could use spiritual occult powers to obtain what you want in an unjust manner, you will be able to resist the temptation. Develop integrity and justice in every aspect of your life. Do not require it from those who surround you, you should even develop compassion to be able to tolerate the behaviors of others that are not like yours.

You are the one seeking to become a knight of justice, to dominate the reptile instincts, and you should not impose such methods to anyone else. Do not judge others when they are acting with arrogance, vanity or betrayal. Transform yourself into a knight, become a dominator of the animal's behavior, and you will have the freedom to direct its power to your will and command.

Do not forget about your human self. Any sign of arrogance will confirm your loss of control over the human animal. Do not be so pretentious as to believe you have mastered the human animal until you really are a master. Be humble, be happy, breathe deeply and practice diligently.

The fear of elements

Elemental fears and self mastery

The human race has survived all these thousands of years because of its efficient defense mechanisms. The process of fear was, for a long time, an essential ingredient to survival. With time, we grew to become humans with more awareness and intellectual development. Still, we are stuck with the animal behaviors of before. These behaviors are major obstacles to our self development, and they hinder the opening of the energy vortexes that are needed to channel more energy through our bodies.

The fear of fire is strong enough to incapacitate us when we are confronted with a flame bigger than we can usually manage. Of course, we are using stoves and ovens, candles, fireplaces, but our fear of fire is still there.

A lot of people are afraid of heights, and a few of high winds. Others are afraid of water itself, or afraid to touch the bottom of a lake with their naked feet. Our fears of the elements run deeper than we think. Before you say you are not afraid of water, ask yourself if you can stay 30 seconds without any equipment, sitting 12 feet deep on the mushy bottom of a lake? Before you say you are not afraid of winds, did you ever skydive, many times? Our fear of earth is also related to the fear of dark closed areas, like being alone for an hour in a dark cave.

Besides the physical manifestation of the elements, there is also an emotional aspect of our elemental fears. Our fear of earth is our fear of being left alone, and of being left without enough substance to survive. Our fear of water is our jealousy, our need to be desired and to possess control over others. Our fear of air is both our feeling of superiority and inferiority. Our fear of fire is our fear of anger and violence.

Our physical bodies contain programmed reactions called instincts. Our instinct is both a valuable tool of prediction, and a trap of fear. It was important, once, to do all in our power to protect our capacity to reproduce and to raise a family. For this, we developed jealousy, possessiveness, and aggressive reactions to competition. We also did all that we could to accumulate physical goods to provide for the periods of need. Envy pushed the strongest to become kings. Ambition was under the control of the animal mind. As long as you cling to these past genetic human reactions, you will create pain in your heart. These instincts are there to help you, not to hinder your development.

To augment your energy flow, with intensity and magnitude, you must go over your animal fears to become aware of them. Don't be a fool and throw yourself in a burning fire, just to prove to yourself that you are not afraid of fire anymore. Defeating a fear does not imply becoming stupid and risking your life over it. Take the time to look at your behaviors, and try to identify which are not useful anymore.

When you notice you act like a hypocrite, or a manipulator, do not judge yourself too harshly. These behaviors were necessary for a long time so that our race could survive. Thus, forgive yourself and work at becoming a better person.

The rectification of your behaviors can take quite a lot of time before they go away, since they have been there for thousands of years, transmitted from parent to cub, then from parent to child. Never think you are above all of this. Your human body is still an animal. Self mastery starts with the humility to accept the point where you now stand, and the courage to look towards your next step.

Defeating the fear of the elements

Amongst the different fears we have, the fear of the elements is an obstacle to our self realization. We believe that fire is our worst fear, but earth, water and wind also hide their share of threat. To overcome our fears of the elements, we must first understand them.

During the following experiences, when fears rise to the surface, breathe deeply and take a few seconds, or even a minute, to feel the fear and what is behind it. Feel your emotions and let it all awake, while you are breathing softly.

Our basic fear of fire is simple to grasp: it can injure us badly. Since we are afraid of fire, we tend not to get close to it, even if a little closer wouldn't hurt us, we stay as far as we can, to be certain that we won't get hurt. This is a problem in itself, because we do not evaluate our behavior according to good discernment but we remain submitted to an animal genetic reaction.

To master the fire, of course, we must not get hurt. But we must make experiments to see how close we could get without hurting ourselves. Start with a single candle and pass your hand over it quickly, then slowly, then closer, and experiment the feeling until it burns to the point of un-comfort. Do not endure to the point of hurting yourself. The goal is to develop self mastery, not to be a masochist. Hurting yourself is a lack of love for your body.

After you know your limits with a candle, get your hands close to burning logs in a fire. Don't be afraid to take a log by one cool end, if the other end is red hot. The goal, again, is to gain self mastery. If you hurt yourself, you are not mastering yourself. Be careful. You want to break the animal genetic reaction of the human body and still be able to ensure your safety by becoming aware of your limits.

Learning how to spit fire from a master of this art is the next step. One day, you might even wish to take a fire walk initiation. Do not do this alone, ever. It has to be passed by initiation.

Concerning the fear of air, going way up in a tower with protection will help you reveal some fear of heights. Going up with less protection will reveal more. Do not play with your life, but play with your fear. Be reasonable, conscious, and develop self mastery, not self stupidity. Be careful and trigger your fear. Be aware of the emotions that rise, and breathe them in. The next step would be sky diving.

With the fear of water come the fear of depth and the fear of dying. Practice yourself at diving underwater, then under more water. Practice keeping your breath for a few seconds more each time. With time, you will sit on the bottom of a pool or a lake, 10 feet deep, and rest there for 20 second before you rise up again. After that, you are simply developing your diving ability, which has nothing to do with our current matter at hand, but it can be good for you. Be aware of your emotions. When you get back up to the surface, breathe to get your oxygen, but also to be aware of your emotions.

With the fear of earth will come the fear of deep, dark places. Practice yourself at being alone for 30 minutes in a pitch black dark room, with absolutely no sound. Breathe softly to make as little sound as you can. If you can find a safe way to go into a cave, go there in the middle of the night, with light only to travel. Stay a while in a pitch black environment, like a deep forest, on a night with no moon. After a while, practice spending a few hours, or a few days completely alone with nothing to do. Try spending a few days without a single sound coming out of your mouth, complete silence, with no music, and no close river to listen to.

With all these experimental quests, you should get to know yourself better, to know your limits and to understand the genetic origins of your fears. It is essential to experience all of these before you get to master the elements, and call the elemental spirits to manifest in your presence.

Of the spirit

Meditation

The Light is everywhere, the Light is everything

Sit down, cross-legged. Breathe deeply and relax. Think of the quantum physics "unified field" if you know about it. Think about the energy inside everything, smaller than the atom, to initiate a state of mind, a contemplation of the base of creation. Remember that the Light is everywhere, the Light is everything. Breathe deeply for a minute. Place your hands in the meditation gesture, both palms up, one hand resting over the other, with your two thumbs touching lightly. Keep your spine erected, but without strain.

"Light is everywhere", spoken in your mind. Think of your immediate environment, and think of your own body. "Light is everything", spoken in your mind. Think of the composition of what surrounds you, and the composition of your body, at the atomic level. Contemplate that everything is made out of energy.

Matter is made out of energy. Energy is made out of even finer energy. Contemplate the microcosmic truth of fabrication.

Softly breathe white light into your body.

After a few minutes of breathing in light, filling your body with white light, contemplating "Light is everywhere, Light is everything", focus on the mantra "AUM". Repeat the "AUM" within softly, and know it is at the base of creation. Keep repeating the mantra for a while, as long as you wish. Keep in mind the basic thought of "everywhere" and "everything". Let your mind fade in the absolute infinity.

When you are done with your meditation, repeat a few times "Light is everywhere, Light is everything", so that it will become a part of your physical day-to-day life as well as in your meditative state. Open your eyes, stand up, move a bit and repeat the phrase while you start moving again in the physical world. Progressively, this meditation will give you a more tangible access to your ability to manifest.

Yéouan technique

The Yéouan technique is a simple method to make the energies vibrate in your body. It is used as a base to practice your voice for vocalization, and it will also develop your psychic abilities. These seed sounds: Y, É, O, Ou, A and N are six phonetics that are the key to making your energy system vibrate. Each is associated with what is called a "chakra" in the oriental esoteric system. Each chakra is a level of perception of your soul. These simple vocalization exercises will prepare you for higher energies to flow through your body.

Basic mantras

Y

The "ee" in speed.
Associated with the third eye chakra, in the forehead, this sound will trigger the development of perception and accuracy. With time, it will develop clairvoyance.

É

The "ey" in "Hey", the "é" in resumé.
Associated with the throat chakra, at the base of the throat, this sound will trigger the development of communication, and clairaudience, the ability to hear the spiritual planes.

O

Associated with the heart chakra, it will develop intuition.

U

The "oe" in "shoes", the "ew" in "few".
Associated with the solar plexus, it will develop empathy, telepathy and strengthen your aura.

A

Associated with the hara, just below the navel, will enhance your energy level, will trigger the development of memory and the ability to recall past souvenirs (we mean way past souvenirs).

N

Associated with the base chakra, at the bottom of the spine, it will ground the other vowels and awaken your general energy systems.

The "R" is a vibrating sound that will activate your chakras in rotating energy circulations and the "SH" will fill your chakras with life force. For telepathy, use "RUSH". For clairvoyance, use a long stretched "RISHI". Experiment with the different possible combinations and, if possible, feel the movement of the energy in your chakras.

When you vocalize these mantras, stretch them over an entire breath out.

RRRRRRRRRRRRUUUUUUUUUUSHSHSHSHSHSHSH

RRRRRRRRRRRROOOOOOOOOOOOOOOOOOOOOOOO

When you vocalize each vowel, open your throat widely and find a way to place your tongue and mouth so that you will emit a harmonic metallic sound in the high frequencies of your voice.

This high pitch sound will come with time and practice, and it will be much more efficient.

Basic mantras of the Yéouan technique

Do these mantras all in a row, or 9 times each, and relax. Take a deep breath and stretch each mantra as long as you can while the sound is still clear. Vocalize loudly, if you can, without disturbing anyone. No one should hear you chant mantras. Relax before and after you do the mantras. You can accompany this practice with calm meditation.

Focus on your energy body
IIIIIIIIIIIIIIIIIIIIIIIÉÉÉÉÉÉÉÉÉÉOOOOOOOOOOUUUUU
UUUAAAAAAAANNNNNNNN

Focus on your third eye
RRRRRRRRRRRIIIIIIIIIIIIIIIIIIIIIIIIIIIIIIIIIIIIIIIIIIIIIIIIIIIIIII

Focus on the base of your throat
RRRRRRRRRRRÉÉÉÉÉÉÉÉÉÉÉÉÉÉÉÉÉÉÉÉÉÉÉÉÉÉÉÉ

Focus on your heart
RRRRRRRRRRRROOOOOOOOOOOOOOOOOOOOOOOO

Focus on your solar plexus

RRRRRRRRRRRUUUUUUUUUUUUUUUUUUUUUUU

Focus on your hara (below the navel)

RRRRRRRRRRRRAAAAAAAAAAAAAAAAAAAAAAAA

Focus on your base chakra

NNNNNNNNNNNNNNNNNNNNNNNNNNNNNNNNNN

Yéouan application to develop psychic abilities

To develop your psychic abilities, you must do more than use the good mantra and the good colors. You also have to open your mind, elevate your consciousness and free yourself of your fears. The "R" will vibrate with the tip of the tongue close to the front of your mouth. The "S" is like the rattlesnake hissing. It will call the energy of the snake within to enhance the "perception". While you do these practices, you must also be aware of your environment, to keep yourself grounded in the physical plane. It is not elsewhere that you wish to develop yourself.

General body of light

See a white light egg shape all around you, about 3 feet radius from your body. The white light is swirling, moving. Light at the center of your body goes up, and emanates through the top of your head like a fountain of light. It falls down all around you, and when it goes lower than your feet, it curls back under your body to get up through your feet, raises up to your body to continue the cycle. Your body of light is filled with white light. Invoke your God to fill you with compassion, and vocalize the mantra:

IIIIIIIIIIIIÉÉÉÉÉÉÉOOOOOOUUUUUUAAAAANNNNN

Telepathy

Your third eye emits and your solar plexus receives. Stop pointing your finger at others. Stop blaming others for what happens in your life. Be aware of your responsibility to make your life better.

Focus on your third eye
RRRRRRRRRRRRIIIIIIIIIIIIIIIIIIIIIIIIIIISSSSSSSSSSSSSSSSSSSSS
9 times

Focus on your solar plexus

RRRRRRRRRRRRUUUUUUUUUUSSSSSSSSSSSSSSSSSSSS

9 times

Start over with the third eye mantra. You will develop quickly with 30 minutes a day. Your mind might go wild a bit. Do not try to stop your thoughts because it's impossible. Simply don't pay attention to them and relax. Focus on the corresponding chakra when you vocalize.

Clairvoyance

This ability will show images to your imaginative mind. Some images will come from your subconscious mind, some will be your own dreams. Visions are passed through the same cerebral interface as dreams, creativity, and imagination. The only difference is that you are not emitting these images, but they come from themselves. This is why it is hard at first to discern one from another. Take your time. It will come. With a lot of practice, these images will go as far as your cerebral ocular processor, and you will see with your own eyes. To this depth of perception, I consider to be a curse more than a gift, since it is one step before schizophrenia. Be careful to exorcise your inner demons before you get there.

Focus on your third eye

RRRRRRRRRRRIIIIIIIIIIIIIIIIIIIIIIIIISSSSSSSSSSSSSSSSSSSS

Multiple of 9 times

Clairaudience

Take a lot of periods of silence. Give yourself time to relax your sense of hearing as well as your nervous system. Listen to silence, and let your ear perceive the sounds from within, and from above. Then do the mantras for a while, and return to silence.

Focus on the base of your throat

RRRRRRRRRRRÉÉÉÉÉÉÉÉÉÉÉÉÉÉÉÉSSSSSSSSSSSSSSSSSSSS

Multiple of 9 times

Intuition

Intuition will grow as you learn to love people unconditionally. Develop compassion and forgive those who hurt you. It does not mean they were right to do what they did. It simply means you wish to stop hurting yourself with what they did. Know that everyone here is in a big collective experience. Intuition will come.

Focus on your heart
RRRRRRRRRRRROOOOOOOOOOOOOSSSSSSSSSSSSSSSSSS
Multiple of 9 times

Awaken past lives, memory, collective unconscious

Information from your past lives is still hidden somewhere in you. To awaken this knowledge, you have to go back in your present life. Start by doing a series of the mantra below. Then get into a callback session.

Remember something you did today. Then something you did last week. Then an event that occurred last month, last year, a few years ago… way down to your birth. With each phase, the more important the souvenir was, the more intense the awakening of your past lives will be. With practice, you can awaken souvenirs buried before your birth, maybe on your last deathbed. Then further, and let your higher consciousness guide you from there on. The more important the souvenirs of your present life are awakened, the more powerful will be the effect. Do not try to jump over a bad souvenir of your present life. Be responsible and recognize the truth of your past. Forgive yourself. Then, do the mantra again.

Focus on your hara

RRRRRRRRRRRRAAAAAAAAAAASSSSSSSSSSSSSSSSSSSSS

Multiple of 9 times

In the world

The Calling of Justice

Mantra

EL

Hesed

Tzadkiel

Hachmalim

Tzedek

Bah Kan, Bah poh

The above mantras call the God consciousness, the goodness, the Archangel of Justice, the dominations of the universe, the energy of the planet Jupiter, to come into your life, into where you are, into your body. After three recitations, pray to God to bring goodness and justice into your life, to set the path right, to pay your karma, to relieve you of the weight of sin, or anything in this manner that corresponds to your religion of preferred belief.

Then recite the mantras again. Simply set your human self in tune with the Divine Justice.

Application

Sometimes, you may get into situations of life that you believe to be unequal, not done with integrity. This technique will be especially efficient if someone is not honest with you, or is stealing your rights.

Invoke the Divine Justice to be with you. After three invocations, explain the situation to God. Use precise and clear phrases. Tell God about the details without stretching yourself. Do not lose the focus that you are in a spiritual practice. Do not start to play the "victim" to God. Explain, describe the situation and your feeling, be concise. Do not extend the explanation over more than 1 minute.

Be very careful about your attitude. You will be struck with the Justice of God, whatever your opinion of what is right and what is wrong. Do not fear God out of panic, but have a respectful humble attitude. Know that you are little before God, even though he loves you in the fullest. Once the situation is explained, visualize it before you, and place both your hand in front of you, palms facing forward. Recite the mantras three times, without the

"Bah Kan, Bah poh", and continue with the command of manifestation.

"EL, Hesed, Tzadkiel, Hachmalim, Tzedek (3 times), manifest your Divine Justice into my life, in this situation involving <names of all involved, starting with yours if applicable...>, set the experience right according to your Divine Law, move the universe as you please."

Visualize strongly, with willpower, the blue movements of the universe penetrating your experience before you, penetrating the scene with its intensity. Do not visualize the solution of the problem. Do not decide what God will make out of this experience.

Visualize for one minute. Then, invoke the Divine Justice once more, one time, to put your mind and heart in a state of gratitude towards God and his work: "EL, Hesed, Tzadkiel, Hachmalim, Tzedek, thank you, my destiny is in your hands". And meditate for a while, forget about your situation, be thankful that God takes care of you in his own way.

Afterwards, repeat three calm "Todah", to say thank you. In your daily life, do all that you can to resolve the problem, and God will be with you in every situation.

This simple practice is a prayer and an introduction to meditation. It will make you more available to justice and peace in your life. It is good to enhance this practice with the complete ritual of justice, in the next chapter.

Translation

EL = personal God consciousness

Hesed = Glorious light

Tzadkiel = Bringer of right

Hachmalim = The many Mechanisms of the universe

Tzedek = Jupiter planet energies

Bah Kan, Bah poh = Come here, come in this place

Todah = Thank you

Ritual of Justice

If you already have a circle drawn on the floor, it is good. If you don't have an "occultum" ready, it doesn't matter. You can have candles lit and incense burning if you wish, but is not necessary in the day-to-day practice.

Place 4 Blue and 4 violet candles, in a circle around you.

Have odors or incense of lavender and Ylang-Ylang.

Ritual - part one

See everything as blue around you and say these mantras:

EL

Hesed

Tzadkiel

Hachmalim

Tzedek

Stand up. Chant the above series of mantra 4 times, and on the fourth time, you will continue with the invocation:

(EL, Hesed, Tzadkiel, Hachmalim, Tzedek x 4)... bring your divine justice into my life.

Repeat the four series of mantra and the incantation of justice four times all together. Thru this invocation, you will call a total of 16 times this set of names of God in his goodness and peace aspects.

Continue with this prayer: "As above, so below, as below, so above. I have a mother and a father in the heavens. El, Hesed, Tzadkiel, cleans my soul, fill my soul with light, make me free, give me the understanding of divine justice, and the power to rectify my path."

Ritual - part two

See everything become red light around you. Take a few deep breaths and continue with the following mantras:

Elohim Gibor

Geburah

Kamael

Seraphim

Maadim

Do this series of mantra 5 times and finish with "... bring your divine justice into my life, rectify everything, and ... " ask your request here. Repeat the 5 series of mantra and the incantation 5 times, totaling 25 series of mantras.

Ritual - part three

Sit down. Get into a meditative state. Recite the mantras of the first part slowly, a few times without counting, while seeing everything blue. Then, recite the mantras of the second part slowly, while seeing everything red. Keep on for a few minutes, alternating between the two sets of mantras. This will activate the power of Divine Justice into your life. As you do the third part of the ritual, forget about your precise request, and let God work into your life.

Translation

EL = my God consciousness

Hesed = Glorious light

Tzadkiel = Bringer of right

Hachmalim = The many Mechanisms of the universe

Tzedek = Jupiter planet energies

Elohim Gibor = Lords of Strength

Geburah = Strength / severity

Kamael = He is the Archangel of Action and War.

Seraphim = The forces of the universe

Maadim = Mars planet energies

Mystical quantum physics

The string theory

As quantum physic evolves, researchers are discovering a universal truth behind all particles, called the string theory. This theory scientifically explains what is beyond every type of particle. We once thought that the atom was the smallest particle that existed, but then we saw that the atom was made of even smaller particles, called protons, neutrons and electrons. We then saw that protons and neutrons were made out of small particles called quarks.

Depending on the orientation of quarks, it would make a proton or a neutron. We thought for a while that quarks were the smallest existing particle, but other types of particles were discovered, that did not even have mass, so small and without form. Up to 12 particles were discovered, and their anti-particle equivalents, called anti-matter.

The string theorists discovered that each of these particle types were made out of an even finer and smaller thing; a single string of energy vibrating like the strings on a violin. A string can vibrate in many ways, and each way produces a type of particle that will then form matter, atoms, molecules, etc…

The reason for our interest in the string theory of quantum physics is because of its spiritual compatibility. The string theory proves that matter in every way is made out of a vibration of un-created energy. This energy is the origin of everything in the known universe, and it is not physical. Physical matter is only a vibration of energy that keeps its position in space because it is "remembering" its pattern of vibration (this is a metaphor, of course). Physical matter is not solid, as we once thought. The Buddhists knew that matter does not really exist, that it is made out of energy, originatingd from spirit. Meanwhile, the Kabalists explain the universe as a vibration of the name of God.

Another interesting fact is quantum mechanics. The string theory at last explained that the universe does not only comprise three dimensions, but ten. Three that are physical, our physical world, one time-dimension, and 6 other dimensions bent in each particle. There is also a kabalistic rule stating that the universe is made out of 10 spheres of existence, that the dimensions are ten, no more, no less. For thousands of years, since Abraham and Moses, the quantum physics of the mystics is based on what today's scientists have discovered.

You can practice the "tree of life chant" to help your consciousness become aware of, and understand the occult knowledge behind the quantum physics theory.

The malleable world

The Light is everywhere, the Light is everything. Contemplation of this thought will help you conceive in your mind the forces behind the atoms, the force that moves the universe itself, like titans pushing the cosmic wheel. Imagine flows of physical and ethereal energy, light in motion like streams in the vastness of the world that moves the winds, makes the rock stay put, and pushes the water in lakes. Transpose this vision at the planetary level, with forces pushing the magma within the earth, and the rotation of the planets around the sun, and the magnetic forces coming from the sun to heat the earth.

Take a bit of time to ponder this vision. Breathe smoothly and relax. See these forces taking the shape of very subtle winds, like veiled streams of energy. These forces are alive and intelligent. As you breathe, imagine that your slow breathing is the movement of the cosmic Life. You encompass the universe within your breath, with majestic movement of the cosmic Life. Take some time to attune yourself to this feeling, forget yourself in the universal breath.

After a while, penetrate the sub-atomic level of matter, and see how malleable it is, how it is made out of energy, flexible, transformable. Matter is not hard and stiff like you perceive at a human level, but it is changing, energy with bonds, that bend, re-adapt, renew, re-link, re-size... The mass of matter does not exist, everything is made out of energy at the essential base, and creation is changing. The energy that makes physical matter does not believe in its constancy in shape, only we believe this, as humans. The matter knows it is energy, and that it is flexible and malleable.

Imagine that all things are liquid, all physical matter is transformable, changeable, and that it obeys the force of the Life that molds it. Breathe with the universal movement of creation, the malleable energy at the base of everything. As you breathe, everything becomes white, as you get to perceive only the essential energy flow of the created universe, flexible, always in motion, white pure essence. Bathe in this white light, the Light is everywhere, the Light is everything.

The power of manifestation

Heaven on earth, veiled by the human mind

"What is above is like what is below, and what is below is like what is above, to accomplish the miracles of one same thing."

— Hermes Thot

All is the same, all is one. The physical plane of existence is like the spiritual planes of existence in an allegoric manner. Heaven is earth, not somewhere else, but here. All that you will see of heaven will depend on your perception of life. Your power of manifestation will be determined by your ability to see in your life the possible wonders of heaven before they actually manifest before you. In fact, everything is ready to be shown, but waiting for the correct moment for you to be able to perceive it. You must convince yourself that heaven on earth is possible, or you will not develop the power of manifestation.

Put some smiles in your life. Smile to anyone at anytime. Do not make a fool of yourself if you are not ready to assume the consequences, but you can smile in a polite and respectful manner to anyone who would look at you. Smiling will produce happiness in your life automatically. It will stimulate the secretion of the correct hormones in the brain to modify the perception you have of life in a positive way.

The human mind perceives its immediate universe in the way it chose, or was conditioned to perceive it. Heaven is nowhere else than earth, but so is hell. All takes place in this wonderful world of manifestations. If you become a master of this perception filter, removing the veil over the human mind, you will be able to access the power of manifestation and define your own reality in any way you chose. We are not talking in illusion here, or convincing ourselves of a better dream. We are talking about the actual modification of events that concern your human experience; true manifestation power. The greatest masters even modify the substance of matter to modify it into something else.

Smile, breathe deeply, make yourself happy and available to see heaven on hearth, and you will see it. This is the fist key in opening the doors of Spirit on earth. Visualize yourself emanating smiles and rays of golden joy that glow and vibrate from all of your body. Keep your head straight, without arrogance, and be happy. Do not over do it, like if you played a role in a piece of theater, but do it for real. Make yourself happy with your willpower and visualize the happiness flowing through you.

Know that there is hell on earth, so that you are not deceived when you seek heaven and get face to face with a manifestation from hell. Look at hell, and know that there is also heaven, and that you are happy in your immediate universe.

Do not let yourself be distracted by ugliness and hatred. Be responsible for your actions, solve your problems in the best of your ability and keep focusing on heaven on earth. This method will open the access for your Spirit to manifest in your physical daily life.

Synchronizing heaven and earth

The root of the universe is above, not below. The highest rate of energy vibration is the base of creation, the origin. From the absolute truth, the light came down and shined into the void, filling it with its light. The universe is filled from above with the highest vibration, which is then coagulated, slowing its vibration rate, agglutinating particles of light together to become shapes and forms. This manifestation takes place through the entire universe. Everywhere, there is a fully vibrating light source, and then all the planes of existence, and then there is physical matter. There is not a point in the physical universe where the origin took place, and that would be the only place to find the highest vibration. The full truth is everywhere, the highest source is everywhere, and if the origin of the universe came from a single point, then the entire universe is this single point.

The mistake that came with the categorization of the planes and dimensions is the belief that they are all separated by some sort of veil, or that they are at different places. Every level of vibration is at exactly the same place as the other levels of vibration. Every plane exists everywhere. Another mistake is to believe that there are definite separations from plane to plane. Like if there was a wall, a barrier between planes. Every plane is at the same place, in the same dimension. We can even say that there is only one plane that vibrates at every level of frequency.

We have decided that from this frequency to that frequency, the energy is classified in one single isolated plane. The planes are not definite and rigid. We have classified them so that we could understand, but in reality, there is no plane. At every point into the universe, every level of frequency exists. An angel, elemental spirit and a human being are exactly in the same dimension, at the same place. If a spiritual being would have a denser body, our human senses could perceive it. If we would be aware at a higher vibration rate, we would see and interact with an angel, because he is not in another dimension, he is at the same place, but only on a higher frequency.

Stop separating the planes of existence. Stop defining the different dimensions with such precision. There are different beings, living in bodies of different frequency of matter, at the same place, time, and dimension. There is only a difference in frequency. If a spiritual entity would take a denser/slower frequency level, it could interact with physical matter, and we might be able to see its shape.

What we do when we summon a spirit is that we gather denser matter for the spirit to take as a body, so that it can interact with us. If we are able to gather a lot of energy at many levels of frequency, from highest to lowest possible, we could provide an ethereal and physical body to a spirit and let it manifest physically. Usually, we are able to gather astral, and a bit of ethereal energy, so the contact is of less importance.

Like with the air over the surface of water, the pressure difference between the two densities of matter will produce some kind of subtle wall. We call this the surface retention property. Between two masses of matter of different density, there is a partial hardening of the contact surface between the two masses. This phenomenon is the same with frequency levels in the planes of existence. This wall is not impermeable, hard and fixed. It is flexible, and it is not composed of any matter at all. It is an illusion produced by difference. Like on the surface of water, we might see a mirror of what is above, and not be able to see through, to look under the surface of water. This phenomenon is also applicable to planes of existence. It is an illusion of optics, hiding the treasures of the next plane, but we must keep in mind that this veil does not exist; it is composed of nothing.

The method

To synchronize heaven and earth, you must first remember that every vibration level exist at any given point in the universe. Focus on this thought, and do a simple energy gathering technique, with the awareness of the continuity of frequencies. Breathe in and out, with energy flowing in your body. Imagine that your physical body is vibrating energy, and that you exist simultaneously at every level of vibration. At the same place, your body is matter, ether, emotional, mental, spiritual... divine vibration, in a beautiful gradient of vibrations. It is not a bunch of fixed vibration levels, but a full spectrum of frequencies, without definite separations.

Building the laboratory

The laboratory is the mystical place where you will operate the manifestations. It is not a place in the 3rd dimension, but a place in the other continuous levels of vibration, that we call planes. On each plane, you will gather energy masses of raw matter, around and inside you, so that you can project a materialization of energy from the spiritual planes to the physical. If, at any plane, the energy is insufficient, the manifestation will not occur, or it could take much more time to operate the manifestation.

At the highest planes, the laboratory is always around you, not even concerned by the position in physical space. For the denser planes, the position in space might be important if you want to gather immense masses of energy for multiple manifestations, or for a quick manifestation. It is recommended not to define a single place where you could manifest, and simply re-gather the denser levels of matter around you when you want to manifest. Nonetheless, this place could be where you have your own personal altar. The denser the energies, the more it is influenced by its physical position. The subtle energies are more influenced by its source and origin, its concept, its goal.

The method

Start with at least 5 minutes of synchronizing heaven and earth. There is an available energy particle of every frequency, everywhere. Fell it, first in your body, but eventually you will feel it at every level of vibration.

Once your mind and body is synchronized and connected with the energy reality, you will gather the raw matter of creation around you. Each breathe in gathers energy from every level around and inside you. Each breath out intensifies the masses of white light around you. Do not force the phenomena. See it, want it, believe it, know it, visualize it. Relax your body, breathe in slowly and breathe out slowly. The operation is not done by forcing the energy level to change, but by collaboration of wills. At each breath in, see more and more energy coming from the highest frequency level of the universe, willingly pouring down more energy into the universe, especially while you gather it consciously.

The flow of energy is not from one place to another lower place, like a physical river, but from one energy level to another lower energy level, everywhere. It is always white light, always pure untouched energies, ready to receive a manifestation model at every level of its existence. It is more than energy, it is Life. It is all the kabbalistic sephiroth at the same time, it is all the planes at once, but always pure light, directly from the source.

Some mantras and divine words augment greatly this process, but require an initiation to be transmitted, since it is not intellectual knowledge, but rather a lived experience. However, it is not required to receive these initiations to be able to construct an efficient laboratory. More powerful than any mantra, the virtues of faith and hope will build the best laboratory.

Even if it is never used to actually operate a definite process of manifestation, your laboratory's energy will always be available to you, and will provide an extra touch to each one of your practices.

The operation of manifestation

The advanced spiritualist will understand that this operation cannot be thought with speech or writing, but the greater outlines can be revealed. The actual refinements of the operation will be discovered through contemplation of the universal truth.

The power to manifest belongs to God only. Humans can transform, can use parts of energy from one aspect and make it into another, can rearrange and recompose, but only God creates new unused matter or energy. The human can contemplate a subject of manifestation and project it into the raw matter of creation. This operation is called "projection". It consists on aligning the 4 planes of human existence into a single conception representing the object of manifestation. This conception aligned with the spirit will pass from the higher planes of consciousness to the lower planes of manifested existence, manifesting the defined conception.

1- The mind must define clearly the subject of manifestation.
2- The emotions must calmly desire, and feel the concept of the subject of manifestation.
3- The will must be calm but strong, with self-confidence, trust, and faith.
4- There must be a physical representation of the subject of manifestation, either in movement, or in correspondence.

The spirit will be aligned with the universal truth. The universal force and substance of the world, with the cosmic Life and it's breath, will be moving to fill the shape defined by every plane and aspect of the conception. White light will take the shape of the conception, and it will conceive.

There are great secrets hidden in this little article, hidden as well in the Emerald Table of Hermes Thot. Understand every aspect of the art, experiment with integrity and keep your heart lifted towards God.

Once you understand the fundamentals of this operation, you will have the power to manifest, but remember that only God creates. After your first successful manifestation, do not give your human ego the credit for the manifestation, but give it to God. You may congratulate yourself for your perseverance, but until you are a true master of the art, you are never to speak about it or share your experience with anyone else. This would automatically attract a karmic weight to your soul, and prevent any further manifestation until the dept of arrogance is paid.

Meditate every aspect of the art, and listen inside for the revelation of your Divine Spirit, for this information that cannot be passed by human-to-human communication, for the knowledge that is beyond possible human thought. Then, define your conception and repeat the operation with a calm, peaceful and powerful attitude. If you ask any question about the operation, then you have not yet discovered the power to do so. Study, listen, and expand your consciousness.

Rituals

When we say "God", we wish to refer to your belief of an absolute energy or intelligence behind everything. You should replace it with the name or concept of your choice. The goal is to open your self to a higher cause so that the ritual will be efficient. These rituals can be done alone or in a group. Learn every aspect of a ritual before you practice it. The more correspondences you join in the application of a method, the more efficient it will become.

Prayer of the seven seals

I trust myself,

I have faith in God,

My path is blessed.

I am happy,

I live in compassion and

I desire peace.

I am tolerant,

I seek justice.

I am strong,

Humbly,

I love.

I am prudent,

I keep hope,

I reside in God.

Everywhere I look,

My face spreads the Great Joy,

And, step-by-step, I come back home.

Amen.

Basic Kabalah training

The kabalistic cross

This ritual will create an expansion in your bodies of light. It will make the flow of spiritual energies stronger and install the symbol of a cross in your aura, calling blessings and evolution forever. It takes only a few minutes, and brings good benefits. Do it also before the "lesser banishing pentagram ritual".

In Kabalah practices, when you say a word, you also vibrate it. You have to imagine the word emanating its sound waves strongly on the energy and astral planes, taking a shape of light. Put your will into it. Decide it strongly and keep a mental focus on the vibrating word. Stay relaxed.

Technique

Stand up towards the East. Imagine that you are getting larger and larger, growing beyond your physical body, growing very large. Visualize yourself standing on the earth. You are very large, becoming a Titan, you are in space, amongst the stars. Visualize a sphere of white light above your head. With your left hand down, palm opened facing forward, place your right thumb over your right two last fingers, keeping the index and major extended. Take a minute to expand, while breathing deeply.

Raise your right hand to your forehead, touching your forehead with your two extended fingers. Say "Athoh" and see a beam of light go from the sphere above your head, upwards to the infinite space. Take a deep breath and vibrate with your mind and will.

Bring your right hand down, touch your lower abdomen while visualizing the beam of light coming from the sphere above your head down through your body, to the earth, downwards forever. As you touch your lower abdomen, say and vibrate "Malkut". Take a deep breath and vibrate with your mind and will.

Bring your hand to your right shoulder. As you touch it, say "Ve Geburah" and visualize your right shoulder shoot an horizontal beam of light to the right. Take a deep breath and vibrate with your mind and will.

Hands to your left shoulder, say "Ve Gedulah" and the beam of light from your right shoulder is also streaming light to the left, reinforced with the light from your left shoulder. Take a deep breath and vibrate with your mind and will. This creates a cross, from the infinite above to the infinite below, from the infinite on the right to the infinite to your left, you are a cross of white light.

Get both your arms up horizontally to make the cross with your entire body, visualizing the beams of light crossing through your arms, and vibrate "Le Olam". Take a deep breath and vibrate with your mind and will.

Get both your hand together at the center of your chest, and say "Amen". Take a deep breath and vibrate with your mind and will. The Hebrew words by themselves are powerful. Understanding them will make your mind contribute to the ritual, making it more efficient.

Translation

Athoh Malkut Ve Geburah Ve Gedulah Le Olam Amen

Athoh: To you
Malkut: the kingdom
Ve Geburah: and the power
Ve Gedulah: and the glory
Le Olam: for eternity
Amen: so be it

To you belongs the kingdom, the power and the glory, for eternity, so be it.

Lesser pentagram banishing ritual

This ritual will clear dense energies and purify the immediate environment for any of your practices. It is a kabbalistic ritual, thus it's efficiency will grow with your knowledge of kabbalah. In the past, it was used to banish demons from a magic circle. It installs a circle around you with calm pure energy.

In the ritual, you will be asked to draw the lesser pentagram in front of you. This is done by extending your index and medium fingers of your right hand, and placing your two last fingers bent under your thumb. Keep your left hand opened, palm facing forward. This way you will be able to draw a 5 pointed start in front of you.

Place your right hand in front of you to your left and down, arm extended, at a point about at the level of your left hip (1), and bit further left of your body. You start on the lower left point, and go up to a point a bit above your head (2). Keep you arm extended. Go down to the lower right point, about at the level of your right hip and a little bit further right of your body (3). Go back to your far left, up at the level of your shoulders (4), and to the far right, still at the level of your shoulders (5). Close the pentagram by going back down again to the lower left point (1).

As you draw the pentagram in front of you, see it drawn on the ethereal and astral plane with beams of white light. You will then place your right hand in the middle of the pentagram, 5 fingers opened, and resonate a name of God with your voice, mind and will power.

The ritual

Face east and do the kabbalistic cross once.

Draw a lower earth banishing pentagram to the east with your index and medium, calmly, and see it glow. Place your hand opened in the center of the pentagram and resonate the name "Yod He Vaw He". As you vibrate this name of God, see a big wave of yellow energy filling all the space before you, the entire east section.

With your hand still in the middle of the pentagram, point your index and medium again in front of you. Keeping your arm straight in front, at the level of your heart, do a quarter of a rotation to your right, turning your entire body to face south. As you turn, you are drawing a bar of energy with the tip of your fingers that will eventually make a full circle around you, when you finish facing each direction.

Bring your pointing finger to the lower right and describe a big pentagram again. Place your open hand in the middle and resonate ADONAÏ. Vibrate the name and feel a burst of red light filling the pentagram and the south section.

Fingers pointed, 90 degree rotation to your right, facing west. Now, half of a circle is drawn around you. Draw a pentagram and resonate EHEIEH (E – HE – IEH). Blue energy fills the west.

Fingers pointed, 90 degrees to your right, facing north, draw another segment of the circle. Draw a pentagram and resonate AGLA (A Ge Le A). Green energy fills the north section.

Fingers pointed again, a last 90 degrees to your right to complete the circle around you with the tip of your fingers. You are facing east again.

Extend your arms on each side to form a Cross with your body. Say the prayer:
Before Me Raphael, (See yellow and violet light in front of you)
Behind me Gabriel, (See blue and orange light behind you)
On my right Michael (See red and green light on your right)
On my left Auriel (See green and brown light on your left)
Before me flames the Pentagram
(See a HUGE pentagram in front of you)
And behind me shines the Six-pointed Star.
(See a HUGE six pointed Star of David)

Do the kabbalistic cross again, and rest.

Middle pilar exercice

Start with the Qabalistic Cross and the Lesser Banishing Ritual of the Pentagram.

Stand up or sit in a comfortable position, while keeping your spine erected straight. Take a few minutes to relax yourself. Breathe deeply. Visualize a glowing ball of light above your head, about 3 inches wide.

Inhale, completely filling your lungs, and continue to visualize the light ball above your head. As you exhale, watch the light growing in brilliance while you vibrate the word "Eheieh", which is the name of God at the Kether Sephira. Repeat this process for a total of ten times. Relax for a few minutes and feel the Energy pulsing in your body and above your head.

Visualize a ray of white Light coming down through your head from the ball of light above your head, down to your throat. Inhale, completely filling your lungs, and visualize a second ball of light in the center of your throat. As you exhale, the ball of light brightens while you vibrate "Yehovah Elohim", which is the name of God at the Daath Sephira (11th sephira of the tree of life, not usually displayed). Repeat this process nine more times. Relax and feel the Energy pulsing in your body.

Visualize a ray of Light coming down through your chest from the ball of light in your throat to the area around your heart and solar plexus. Inhale, completely filling your lungs, and visualize a third ball of light at your heart and solar plexus area. The ball of light brightens as you exhale while vibrating "Eloha Ve-Daath", which is the name of God at the Tipheret Sephira. Repeat this process nine more times. Relax for a few minutes, and scan your body, noticing any change. Feel the Energy pulsing.

Visualize a ray of Light coming down from your chest to your pelvic area. Inhale, completely filling your lungs, and visualize a fourth ball of light around your genitals. The ball of light brightens as you exhale while vibrating "Shadaï EL Haï", which is the name of God at the Yesod Sephira. Repeat this process nine more times. Relax for a few minutes and feel your body.

Visualize a ray of Light coming down from your pelvis to a point beneath your feet. Inhale, completely filling your lungs, and visualize a fifth ball of light beneath your feet. The ball of light brightens as you exhale while vibrating "Adonaï Melek", which is the name of God at the Malkut Sephira. Repeat this process nine more times. Pay attention to your entire body and feel the pulsation of the Energy.

Focus your attention on the ball of light above your head. As you exhale, bring a stream of Light down your left side to the ball of light beneath your feet. Inhale, and bring it back up your right side to the ball of light above your head, forming thereby a Circle of brilliant Light. Repeat this process nine more times.

Focus your attention on the ball of light above your head. Exhale, and bring a stream of Light down the front of your body to the ball of light beneath your feet. Inhale, and bring it back up the rear of your body to the ball of light above your head, forming thereby a Circle of brilliant Light. Repeat this process nine more times. Relax for a few moments and feel yourself inside a sphere of white Light, which envelopes your entire aura.

Focus your attention on the ball of light beneath your feet. Inhale and bring a brilliant ray of Light through your body and up your spine to the ball of light above your head. While exhaling, visualize a fireworks-like explosion of Light that rains gently down upon you and is collected into the ball of light beneath your feet. Repeat this process nine more times. Scan your body once again, noticing whatever is happening there, and feel the pulsation of the Energy for as long as you wish.

Do the Qabalistic Cross and the Lesser Banishing Ritual of the Pentagram. Meditate and relax.

The Tree of life chant

The Kabbalist's tree of life can be spoken as well as drawn. Every sphere of the tree of life has 5 levels of consciousness, and a name for each level. The 5 levels for each of the 10 spheres are to 50 doors of knowledge. With more knowledge of kabbalah, you will get to understand the following chant and it will enhance the flow of spiritual energies in your bodies, physical and spiritual.

The first 10 names are the names of God, showing a side of his face different for each plane of existence. The second are the sephirot, the soul of the universe, or the planes of existence themselves. The third are the names of the Archangels, rulers of the cosmos and the worlds of spirit. The fourth are the types of angelic aids available, and the fifth are the names of the physical/ethereal manifestation, or the intelligent planet spirits.

It is good to start the chant with the kabbalistic ritual of the lesser pentagram. The left column contains the names of God, and so it is the chant. The right column contains the translation, to help you understand. The translation might be inadequate for the profound understanding of the mysteries of the universe. They are here for the beginner to grasp the first steps of kabbalah. Chant the following names with a soft harmony of your choice.

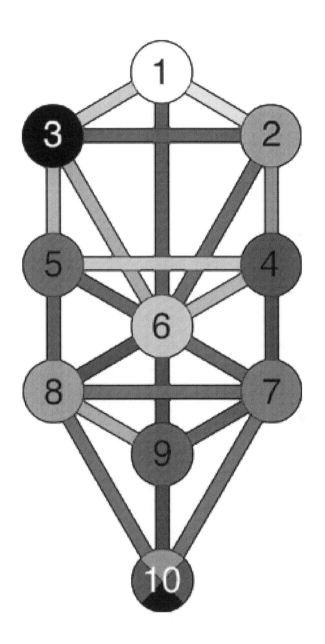

Chant:	Closest meaning:
1- Eheieh	1- Father
2- Iah	2- Christ
3- Yod He Vav He	3- Creator/Holy spirit
4- El	4- God consciousness
5- Elohim Gibor	5- Gods of strength
6- Eloha ve Da-ath	6- God of knowledge
7- Yehovoh Tzebaot	7- Lord of armies
8- Elohim Tzebaot	8- Gods of armies
9- Shadaï El-Haï	9- All mighty God of life
10-Adonaï Melek	10-Lord of the kingdom
1- Kether	1- Crown
2- Hokmah	2- Wisdom
3- Binah	3- Intelligence
4- Hesed	4- Goodness
5- Geburah	5- Force/Strength
6- Tipheret	6- Beauty
7- Netzah	7- Victory
8- Hod	8- Glory
9- Yesod	9- Foundation
10-Malkut	10-Kingdom/physical world

1- Metatron	Archangel name
2- Raziel	Archangel name
3- Tzaphkiel	Archangel name
4- Tzadkiel	Archangel name
5- Kamael	Archangel name
6- Michael	Archangel name
7- Haniel	Archangel name
8- Raphael	Archangel name
9- Gabriel	Archangel name
10-Sandalphon	Archangel name
1- Hayot Ha-Kodesh	1- Holy 4 element spirits
2- Ophanim	2- Original existences
3- Aralim	3- Thrones
4- Hachmalim	4- Dominions
5- Seraphim	5- Powers
6- Malahim	6- Virtues
7- Elohim	7- Leaders/principals
8- Beni-Elohim	8- Archangels
9- Kerubim	9- Angels
10-Ischim	10-Perfect men

1- Reschit Ha-Galgalim	1- First swirls
2- Mazaloth	2- Zodiac
3- Chabtaï	3- Saturn
4- Tzedek	4- Jupiter
5- Maadim	5- Mars
6- Chemesch	6- Sun
7- Noga	7- Venus
8- Kohav	8- Mercury
9- Lenava	9- Moon
10-Olam Yesodoth	10-Earth/eternal manifestation

After chanting the 50 names of God, relax, meditate a little, and start over if you wish. We recommend you drink water before and after each chanting session.

Universal mechanics

Universal mechanics and spirits

In the universe, both physically and spiritually, energy flows following patterns according to the laws of nature. From the smallest levels of atomic activity, to the huge streams of attractive and repulsive pulls of the galaxies, there is an intelligent natural law. These laws, collaborating with one another to manifest the natural experience we perceive, can be accessed and used consciously, with Love as a tool.

These energies and laws are called angels, demons, spirits, titans, gods (as in minor gods), concepts, gravity, electromagnetic forces... all at different levels of density. An angel does not look like a humanoid with wings, it is a force of the universe without shape or name, but like any type of cosmic force, it triggers a concept into our subconscious mind, so that the human can represent itself the force it is in communication with. This is why all those who have perceived angels see them in mostly the same way, because it is the human ability to transpose the other types of energies as images on the imaginative mind, and makes communication accessible with the contacted energy.

The human mind can perceive any type of spiritual force thru its "diaphane", the imagination's mirror, like a translucent membrane over the cosmic reality. Instead of letting the imagination under the control of the human mind and the ego, it can become free to reflect the subconscious mind's perception of the universal force contacted. This is how we can perceive angels and demons thru our inner eye.

The first step is to use our imagination to set the communication in place. By actively controlling our imagination to direct us in a voluntary dream (visualization), we are triggering a specific contact with our subconscious mind to awaken a channel of communication with an intelligent energy stream of the universe (a spirit or angel). Once we arrive at the contact level, once we successfully opened a channel of communication with the desired concept of the universe, we must become passive and receptive, to let the summoned spirit influence our imagination, so that the answer can be passed back to us in the form of feelings, concepts, sounds or images.

For example, let's take a simple visualization. In a state of half-meditation, see yourself in a calm plain surrounded by forest. This aspect is active control of your dream, not letting anything disturb your imaginative mind. Add to this visualization a big tree in the middle of the plain, with someone seated at its root. Call this tree the "Heart Tree" and the person seated the "Hearted One". You are still in active control, provoking the events, making the dream with your own imagination, and naming the elements yourself, so that the contacted information source is the one you wish. Walk to the Hearted One and great him/her. Now it is very important to become passive, receptive, to let the Hearted One answer by him/herself, so that you will not be in control of the answer. Then ask a question to him/her, with your active imagination, and become passive again, listening, letting the answer come by itself to your mind. It is a dance between the active and the passive, the emitting and the receptive. From time to time, your human ego might want to get in the way, but it is easy to simply get back to the communication process.

Through all the visualizations you do, always keep an active focus at the environment you set in place, so that the spirit/energy/mechanics of the universe that you contact is well established, and the link that you establish remains clear and stable. As you keep the active control of the environment, let the central focus of the scene go as it wishes, letting the spirit/energy/mechanics of the universe transmit through your imagination the answer you asked for. If you keep an active control of the central elements of your experience, you will disturb the base of the message that is sent to you. Keep the link alive by keeping the elements that made the link possible, but let everything else go like it wants to, leaving more place for information to pass. Practice yourself at listening and observing.

In a ritual, with the visualization of symbols, calling the name of spirits or angels, using colored candles and herbal smells, even while standing up and keeping your eyes opened, you are establishing the links in the same way you would with your half-meditative visualization. In the same manner, you must keep a passive and receptive point in your mind so that you are able to perceive the information that will come back from the summoned sprit. With time and practice, the energies will be able to pass thru all of your human planes and manifest even around you, in your immediate environment.

The Arbatel of Magic

The Arbatel of Magic appeared around 1575. The original Latin version can be found in Heinrich Cornelius Agrippa's "Fourth book of occult philosophy". It was first translated in English by Mr. R. Turner, in 1654. It was used by many renowned occultists with a true faith in God. It is a book of communion with the spirits called "Olympic" that manages the whole of the experiences of creation.

This manual of occult practice is one big step into the art of Theurgia, the Divine Magical art that connects you to the mechanics of the universe. No evil demands can be called to the Olympic Spirits without severe consequences. Any good deed asked to an Olympic Spirit will produce results, quickly or eventually. It is a very good idea to ask the Olympic Spirits for guidance and help in magic practices, before anything else. Do not be greedy, help others, and ask deeds for yourself with no exaggeration.

In any type of invocation, you must gather together physical and psychological correspondences in one single event, to amplify the effect, open the doors wider, make your mind available to the information and make your direct physical environment available to the work of the invoked spirit. The more correspondences you include in your ritual, the more intense will be the invocation and effects. The longer and more detailed the invocation is, the stronger the effect.

Most of all, the development of Virtues are the key element in the power of an invocation. Seek justice and be compassionate to amplify the work of the spirit Bethor in your life. Be kind and generous to amplify the work of Hagith and Och. Be active and prudent to amplify the work of Ophiel. Each invocation is determined by the flow of Virtues in your heart, mind and body.

Each spirit has his affinities and aversions. A correspondence chart was provided after the original text, to help you understand this concept.

The original 1654 English text contains many irregularities that we can attribute to the mistype of old reproduction technologies, and grammatical variations of the time. With great respect to the original English text, we took the initiative to correct a few glitches to help you in your learning process. Still, the most implicated seeker might want to buy a copy of the original text if he really wants to see the original English translation, or learn Latin and acquire the text by Agrippa.

Here follows a transcription of the 1654 English text of the Arbatel of Magic, along with most of the textual irregularities of the time, allowing you to taste the occult flavor of the text.

ארבעתאל

Of the Magic of the Ancients,
The greatest Studie of Wisdom.

In all things, ask counsel of the Lord;
and do not thou think, speak,
or do any thing, wherein
God is not thy counsellor.

Proverbs 11.

He that walketh fraudulently, revealeth secrets: but he
that is of a faithful spirit, concealeth the matter.

ARBATEL of

MAGICK:

or,

The spiritual Wisdom of the Ancients,

as well Wise-men of the people of God,

as MAGI of the Gentiles:
for the illustration of the glory of God,
and his love to Mankinde.

Now first of all produced out of darkness into the light, against all caco-Magicians, and contemners of the gifts of God; for the profit and delectation of all those, who do truely and piously love the creatures of God, and do use them with thanksgiving, to the honour of God, and profit of themselves and their neighbours.

ARBATEL OF MAGICK

Containing nine Tomes, and seven Septenaries of
APHORISMS.

The first is called *Isagoge*, or, A Book of the Institutions of Magick: or 𐤕 𐤕𐤃𐤋𐤌𐤀𐤐𐤊𐤄𐤎 which in fourty and nine Aphorisms comprehendeth, the most general Precepts of the whole Art. The second is Microcosmical Magick, what *Microcosmus* hath effected Magically, by his Spirit and Genius addicted to him from his Nativity, that is, spiritual wisdom: and how the same is effected.

The third is Olympick Magick, in what maner a man may do and suffer by the spirits of *Olympus*.

The fourth is Hesiodiacal, and Homerical Magick, which teacheth the operations by the Spirits called *Cacodæmones,* as it were not adversaries to mankinde.

The fifth is Romane or Sibylline Magick, which acteth and operates with Tutelar Spirits and Lords, to whom the whole Orb of the earth is distributed. This is *valde insignis Magia.* To this also is the doctrine of the *Druids* referred.

The sixth is Pythagorical Magick, which onely acteth with Spirits to whom is given the doctrine of Arts, as Physick, Medicine, Mathematics, Alchymie, and such kinde of Arts.

The seventh is the Magick of *Apollonius,* and the like, and agreeth with the Romane and Microcosmical Magick: onely it hath this peculiar, that it hath power over the hostile spirits of mankinde.

The eighth is Hermetical, that is, Ægyptiacal Magick; and differeth not much from Divine Magick.

The ninth is that wisdom which dependeth solely upon the Word of God; and this is called Prophetical Magick.

The first Tome of the Book of

Arbatel of Magick

CALLED

ISAGOGE

In the Name of the Creator of all things both visible and invisible,
who revealeth his Mysteries out of his Treasures to them that call
upon him; and fatherly and mercifully bestoweth those his Secrets
upon us without measure. May he grant unto us, through his
onely-begotten Son Jesus Christ our Lord, his ministring spirits,
the revealers of his secrets, that we may write this Book of
Arbatel, concerning the greatest Secrets which are lawful for man
to know, and to use them without offence unto God. *Amen.*

The first Septenary of Aphorisms.

The first Aphorism.

Whosoever would know Secrets, let him know how to keep secret things secretly; and to reveal those things that are to be revealed, and to seal those things which are to be sealed: and *not to give holy things to dogs, nor cast pearls before swine.* Observe this Law, and the eyes of thy understanding shall be opened, to understand secret things; and thou shalt have whatsoever thy minde desireth to be divinely revealed unto thee. Thou shalt have also the Angels and Spirits of God prompt and ready in their nature to minister unto thee, as much as any humane minde can desire.

Aphor. 2.

In all things call upon the Name of the Lord: and without prayer unto God through his onely-begotten son, do not thou undertake to do or think any thing. And use the Spirits given and attributed unto thee, as Ministers, without rashness and presumption, as the messengers of God; having a due reverence towards the Lord of Spirits. And the remainder of thy life do thou accomplish, demeaning thy self peaceably, to the honour of God, and the profit of thy self and thy neighbour.

Aphor. 3.

Live to thy self, and the Muses: avoid the friendship of the Multitude: be thou covetous of time, beneficial to all men. Use thy Gifts, be vigilant in thy Calling; and let the Word of God never depart from thy mouth.

Aphor. 4.

Be obedient to good Admonitions: avoid all procrastination: accustom thy self to Contancie and Gravity, both in thy words and deeds. Resist temptations of the Tempter, by the Word of God. Flee from earthly things; seek after heavenly things. Put no confidence in thy own wisdom; but look unto God in all things, according to that sentence of the Scripture: *When we know not what we shall do, unto thee, O God, do we lift up our eyes, and from thee we expect our help.* For where all humane refuges do forsake us, there will the help of God shine forth, according to the saying of *Philo.*

Aphor. 5.

Thou shalt love the Lord thy God with all thy heart, and with all thy strength, and thy neighbour as thy self: And the Lord will keep thee as the apple of his eye, and will deliver thee from all evil, and will replenish thee with all good; and nothing shall thy soul desire, but thou shalt be fully endued therewith, so that it be contingent to the salvation of thy soul and body.

Aphor. 6.

Whatsoever thou hast learned, frequently repeat, and fix the same in thy minde: and learn much, but not many things, because a humane understanding cannot be alike capable in all things, unless it be such a one that is divinely regenerated; unto him nothing is so difficult or manifold, which he may not be able equally to attain to.

Aphor. 7.

Call upon me in the day of trouble, and I will hear thee, and thou shalt glorifie me, saith the Lord. For all Ignorance is tribulation of the minde; therefore call upon the Lord in thy ignorance, and he will hear thee. And remember that thou give honour unto God, and say with the Psalmist, *Not unto us, Lord, but unto thy Name give the glory.*

The second Septenary.

Aphor. 8.

Even as the Scripture testifies, that God appointeth names to things or persons, and also with them hath distributed certain powers and offices out of his treasures: so the Characters and Names of Stars have not any power by reason of their figure or pronunciation, but by reason of the vertue or office which God hath ordained by nature either to such a Name or Character. For there is no power either in heaven or in earth, or hell, which doth not descend from God; and without his permission, they can neither give or draw forth into any action, any thing they have.

Aphor. 9.

That is the chiefest wisdom, which is from God; and next, that which is in spiritual creatures; afterwards. in corporal creatures; fourthly, in Nature, and natural things. The Spirits that are apostate, and reserved to the last judgement, do follow these, after a long interval. Sixthly, the ministers of punishments in hell, and the obedient unto God. Seventhly, the Pigmies do not possess the lowest place, and they w ho inhibit in elements, and elementary things. It is convenient therefore to know and discern all differences of the wisdom of the Creator and the Creatures, that it may be certainly manifest unto us, what we ought to assume to our use of every thing, and that we may know in truth how and in what maner that may be done. For truely every creature is ordained for some profitable end to humane nature, and for the service thereof; as the holy Scriptures, Reason, and Experience, do testifie.

Aphor. 10.

God the Father Almighty, Creator of heaven and earth, and of all things visible and invisible, in the holy Scriptures proposeth himself to have an eye over us; and as a tender father which loveth his children, he teacheth us what is profitable, and what not; what we are to avoid, and what we are to embrace: then he allureth us to obedience with great promises of corporal and eternal benefits, and deterreth us (with threatning of punishments) from those things which are not profitable for us. Turn over therefore with thy hand, both night and day, those holy Writings, that thou mayest be happie in things present, and blessed in all eternity. Do this, and thou shalt live, which the holy Books have taught thee.

Aphor. 11.

A number of Four is *Pythagorical,* and the first Quadrate; therefore here let us place the foundation of all wisdom, after the wisdom of God revealed in the holy Scriptures, and to the considerations proposed in Nature.

Appoint therefore to him who solely dependeth upon God, the wisdom of every creature to serve and obey him, *nolens volens,* willing or unwilling. And in this, the omnipotency of God shineth forth. It consisteth therefore in this, that we will discern the creatures which serve us, from those that are unwilling; and that we may learn how to accommodate the wisdom and offices of every creature unto our selves. This Art is not delivered, but divinely. Unto whom God will, he revealeth his secrets; but to whom he will not bestow any thing out of his treasuries, that person shall attain to nothing without the will of God.

Therefore we ought to desire *τὴν πλεονεκτικὴν ἐπιστήμην* from God alone, which will mercifully impart these things unto us. For he who bath given us his Son, and commanded us to pray for his holy Spirit, How much more will he subject unto us the whole creature, and things visible and invisible? *Whatsoever ye ask, ye shall receive.* Beware that ye do not abuse the gifts of God, and all things shall work together unto you for your salvation. And

- 145 -

before all things, be watchful in this, That your names be written in heaven: this is more light, That the spirits be obedient unto you, as Christ admonisheth.

Aphor. 12.

In the Acts of the Apostles, the Spirit saith unto *Peter* after the Vision, *Go down, and doubt not but I have sent them,* when *he* was sent for from *Cornelius* the Centurion. After this maner, in vocal words, are all disciplines delivered, by the holy Angels of God, as it appeareth out of the Monuments of the Ægyptians. And these things afterwards were vitiated and corrupted with humane opinions; and by the instigation of evil spirits, who sow tares amongst the children of disobedience, as it is manifest out of *St. Paul,* and *Hermes Trismegistus.* There is no other maner of restoring these Arts. then by the doctrine of the holy Spirits of God; because true *faith cometh by hearing.* But because thou mayst be certain of the truth. arid mayst not doubt whether the spirits that speak with thee, do declare things true or false, let it only depend upon thy faith in God; that thou mayst say with *Paul, I know on whom I trust.* If no sparrow can fall to the ground without the will of the Father which is in heaven, How much more will not God suffer thee to be deceived, O thou of little faith, if thou dependest wholly upon God, and adherest onely to him?

The Lord liveth; and all things which live, do live in him. And he is truely **יהוה**, who hath given unto all things, that they be that which they are: and by his word alone, through his Son, hath produced all things out of nothing, which are in being. He calleth all the stars. and all the host of heaven by their names. He therefore knoweth the true strength and nature of things, the order and policie of every creature visible and invisible. to whom God hath revealed the names of his creatures. It remaineth also, that he receive power from God, to extract the vertues in nature, and hidden secrets of the creature; and to produce their power into action, out of darkness into light. Thy scope therefore ought to be, that thou have the names of the Spirits, that is, their powers and offices, and how they are subjected and appointed by God to minister unto thee; even as *Raphael* was sent to *Tobias,* that he should heal his father, and deliver his son from dangers, and bring him to a wife. So *Michael,* the fortitude of God governeth the people of God: *Gabriel,* the messenger of God, was sent to *Daniel, Mary,* and *Zachary* the father of *John Baptist.* And he shall be given to thee that desirest him, who will teach thee whatsoever thy soul shall desire, in the nature of things. His ministery thou shalt use with trembling and fear of thy Creator, Redeemer, and Sanctifier, that is to say, the Father, Son, and holy Ghost: and do not thou let slip any occasion of learning and be vigilant in thy calling, and thou shalt want nothing that is necessary for thee.

Aphor. 14.

Thy soul liveth for ever, through him that hath created thee: call therefore upon the Lord thy God, and him onely shalt thou serve. This thou shalt do, if thou wilt perform that end for which thou art ordained of God, and what thou owest to God and to thy neighbour. God requireth of thee a minde, that thou shouldest honour his Son, and keep the words of his Son in thy heart: if thou honour him, thou hast done the will of thy Father which is in heaven. To thy neighbour thou owest offices of humanity, and that thou draw all men that come to thee, to honour the Son. This is the Law and the Prophets. In temporal things, thou oughtest to call upon God as a father, that he would give unto thee all necessaries of this life: and thou oughtest to help thy neighbour with the gifts which God bestoweth upon thee, whether they be spiritual or corporal.

There are seven different governments of the Spirits of *Olympus*, by whom God hath appointed the whole frame and universe of this world to be governed: and their visible stars are ARATRON, BETHOR, PHALEG, OCH, HAGITH, OPHIEL, PHUL, after the *Olympick* speech. Every one of these hath under him a mighty *Militia* in the firmament.

* ARATRON ruleth visible Provinces XLIX.
* BETHOR, XLII.
* PHALEG, XXXV.
* OCH, XXVIII.
* HAGITH, XXI.
* OPHIEL, XIIII.
* PHUL, VII.

So that there are 186 *Olympick* Provinces in the whole Universe. wherein the seven Governours do exercise their power: all which are elegantly set forth in Astronomy. But in this place it is to be explained, in what maner these Princes and Powers may he drawn into communication. *Aratron* appeareth in the first hour of *Saturday*, and very truely giveth answers concerning his Provinces and Provincials. So likewise do the rest appear in order in their days and hours. Also every one of them ruleth 490 yeers. The beginning of their simple *Anomaly*, in the 60 yeer before the Nativity of Christ, was the beginning of the administration of *Bethor*, and it lasted until the yeer of our Lord Christ 430. To whom succeeded *Phaleg*, until the 920 yeer. Then began *Och*, and continued until the year 1410, and thenceforth *Hagith* ruleth untill the year 1900.

Aphor. 17.

Magically the Princes of the seven Governments are called simply, in that time, day and hour wherein they rule visibly or invisibly, by their Names and Offices which God hath given unto them; and by proposing their Character which they have given or confirmed.

The governor **Aratron** hath in his power those things which he doth naturally, that is, after the same manner and subject as those things which in Astronomy are ascribed to the power of *Saturn*.

Those things which he doth of his own free will, are,

1. That he can convert any thing into a stone in a moment, either animal or plant, retaining the same object to the sight.

2. He converteth treasures into coles, and coles into treasure.

3. He giveth familiars with a definite power.

4. He teacheth *Alchymy*, Magick, and Physick.

5. He reconcileth the subterranean spirits to men; maketh hairy men.

6. He causeth one to bee invisible.

7. The barren he maketh fruitful, and giveth long life.

His character.

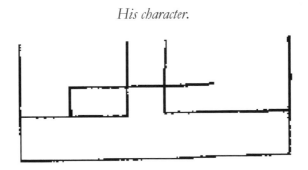

He hath under him 49 Kings, 42 Princes, 35 Presidents, 28 Dukes, 21 Ministers, standing before him; 14 familiars, seven messengers: he commandeth 36000 legions of spirits; the number of a legion is 490.

Bethor governeth those things which are ascribed to *Jupiter:* he soon cometh being called. He that is dignified with his character, he raiseth to very great dignities, to cast open treasures: he reconcileth the spirits of the aire, that they give true answers: they transport precious stones from place to place, and they make medicines to work miraculously in their effects: he giveth also familiars of the firmament, and prolongeth life to 700 yeares if God will.

His character.

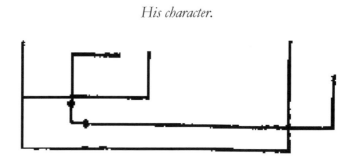

He hath under him 42 Kings, 35 Princes, 28 Dukes, 21 Counsellors, 14 Ministers, 7 Messengers, 29000 legions of Spirits.

Phaleg ruleth those things which are attributed to *Mars*, the Prince of peace. He that hath his character he raiseth to great honours in warlike affaires.

His character.

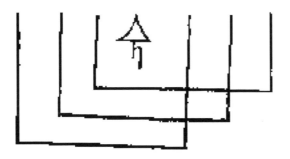

Och governeth solar things; he giveth 600 yeares, with perfect health; he bestoweth great wisdom, giveth the most excellent Spirits, teacheth perfect Medicines: he converteth all things into most pure gold and precious stones: he giveth gold, and a purse springing with gold. He that is dignified with his Character, he maketh him to be worshipped as a Deity, by the Kings of the whole world.

The Character.

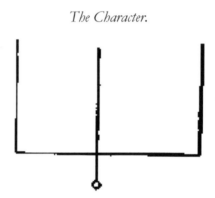

He hath under him 36536 Legions: he administreth all things alone: and all his spirits serve him by centuries.

Hagith governeth *Venereous* things. He that is dignified with his Character, he maketh very fair, and to be adorned with all beauty. He converteth copper into gold, in a moment, and gold into copper: he giveth Spirits which do faithfully serve those to whom they are addicted.

His character.

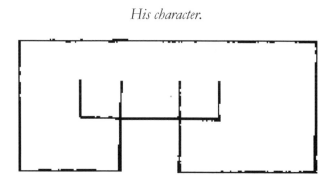

He hath 4000 Legions of Spirits and over every thousand he ordaineth Kings for their appointed seasons.

Ophiel is the governour of such things as are attributed to Mercury: his Character is this.

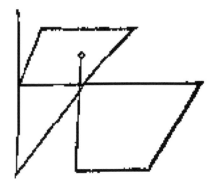

His Spirits are 100000 Legions: he easily giveth Familiar Spirits: he teacheth all Arts: and he that is dignified with his Character, he maketh him to be able in a moment to convert Quicksilver into the Philosophers stone.

Phul *hath this Character.*

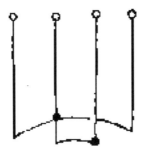

He changeth all metals into silver, in word and deed; governeth Lunary things; healeth the dropsie: he giveth spirits of the water, who do serve men in a corporeal and visible form; and maketh men to live 300 yeers.

The most general Precepts of this Secret.

1. Every Governour acteth with all his Spirits, either naturally, to wit, always after the same maner; or otherwise of their own free-will, if God hinder them not.

2. Every Governour is able to do all things which are done naturally in a long time, out of matter before prepared; and also to do them suddenly, out of matter not before prepared. As *Och*, the Prince of Solar things, prepareth gold in the mountains in a long time; in a less time, by the Chymical Art; and Magically, in a moment.

3. The true and divine Magician may use all the creatures of God, and offices of the Governours of the world, at his own will, for that the Governours of the world are obedient unto them, and come when they are called, and do execute their commands: but God is the Author thereof: as *Joshua* caused the Sun to stand still in heaven.

They send some of their Spirits to the Mean Magicians, which do obey them onely in some determinate business: but they hear not the false Magicians, but expose them to the deceits of the devils, and cast them into divers dangers, by the Command of God; as the Prophet *Jeremiah* testifieth, in his eighth Chapter, concerning the Jews.

4. In all the elements there are the seven Governours with their hosts, who do move with the equal motion of the firmament; and the inferiours do always depend upon the superiours, as it is taught in Philosophy.

5. A man that is a true Magician, is brought forth a Magician from his mothers womb: others, who do give themselves to this office, are unhappie. This is that which *John* the Baptist speaketh of: *No man can do any thing of himself, except it be given him from above.*

Every Character given from a Spirit, for what cause soever, hath his efficacie in this business, for which it is given, in the time prefixed: But it is to be used the same day and Planetary hour wherein it is given.

7. God liveth, and thy soul liveth: keep thy Covenant, and thou hast whatsoever the spirit shall reveal unto thee in God, because all things shall be done which the Spirit promiseth unto thee.

Aphor. 18.

There are other names of the *Olymick* spirits delivered by others; but they onely are effectual, which are delivered to any one, by the Spirit the revealer, visible or invisible: and they are delivered to every one as they are predestinated: therefore they are called Constellations; and they seldome have any efficacie above 40 yeers. Therefore it is most safe for the young practisers of Art, that they work by the offices of the Spirits alone, without their names; and if they are pre-ordained to attain the Art of Magick, the other parts of the Art will offer themselves unto them of their own accord. Pray therefore for a constant faith, and God will bring to pass all things in due season.

Aphor. 19.

Olympus and the inhabitants thereof, do of their own accord offer themselves to men in the forms of Spirits, and are ready to perform their Offices for them, whether they will or not: by how much the rather will they attend you, if they are desired? But there do appear also evil Spirits, and destroyers, which is caused by the envy and malice of the devil; and because men do allure and draw them unto themselves with their sin, as a punishment due to sinners. Whosoever therefore desireth familiarly to have a conversation with Spirits, let him keep himself from enormious [sic] sins, and diligently pray to the most High to be his keeper; and he shall break through all the snares and impediments of the devil: and let him apply himself to the service of God, and he will give him an increase in wisdom.

Aphor 20.

All things are possible to them that believe them, and are willing to receive them; but to the incredulous and unwilling, all things are unpossible [sic]: there is no greater hinderance then a wavering minde, levity, unconstancy, foolish babbling, drunkenness, lusts, and disobedience to the word of God. A Magician therefore ought to be a man that is godly, honest, constant in his words and deeds, having a firm faith toward God, prudent, and covetous of nothing but of wisdom about divine things.

Aphor. 21.

When you would call any of the *Olympick* Spirits, observe the rising of the Sun that day, and of what nature the Spirit is which you desire; and saying the prayer following, your desires shall he perfected.

Omnipotent and eternal God, who hast ordained the whole creation for thy praise and glory, and for the salvation of man, I beseech thee that thou wouldst send thy Spirit N.N. of the solar order, who shall inform and teach me those things which I shall ask of him; or, that he may bring me medicine against the dropsie, &c. Nevertheless not my will be done, but thine, through Jesus Christ thy onely begotten Son, our Lord. Amen.

But thou shalt not detain the Spirit above a full hour, unless he be familiarly addicted unto thee.

Forasmuch as thou camest in peace, and quietly, and hast answered unto my petitions; I give thanks unto God, in whole Name thou camest: and now thou mayest depart in peace unto thy orders; and return to me again when I shall call thee by thy name, or by thy order, or by thy office, which is granted from the Creator. Amen.

Ecclesiast. Chap. 5. *Be not rash with thy mouth, neither let thy heart be hasty to utter any thing before God; for God is in Heaven, and thou in earth: Therefore let thy words be few; for a dream cometh through the multitude of business.*

The fourth Septenary.

Aphor. 22.

We call that a secret, which no man can attain unto by humane industry without revelation; which Science lieth obscured, hidden by God in the creature; which nevertheless he doth permit to be revealed by Spirits, to a due use of the thing it self. And these secrets are either concerning things divine, natural or humane. But thou mayst examine a few, and the most select, which thou wilt commend with many more.

Aphor. 23.

Make a beginning of the nature of the secret, either by a Spirit in the form of a person, or by vertues separate, either in humane Organs, or by what manner soever the same may be effected; and this being known, require of a Spirit which knoweth that art, that he would briefly declare unto thee whatsoever that secret is: and pray unto God, that he would inspire thee with his grace, whereby thou maist bring the secret to the end thou desireth, for the praise and glory of God, and the profit of thy neighbour.

Aphor. 24.

The greatest secrets are number seven.

1. The first is the curing of all diseases in the space of seven dayes, either by character, or by natural things, or by the superior Spirits with the divine assistance.

2. The second is, to be able to prolong life to whatsoever age we please: I say, a corporal and natural life.

3. The third is, to have the obedience of the creatures in the elements which are in the forms of personal Spirits; also of Pigmies,* Sagani, Nymphes, Dryades, and Spirits of the woods.

4. The fourth is, to be able to discourse with knowledge and understanding of all things visible and invisible, and to understand the power of every thing, and to what it belongeth.

5. The fifth is, that a man be able to govern himself according to that end for which God hath appointed him.

6. The sixth is, to know God, and Christ, and his holy Spirit: this is the perfection of the *Microcosmus*.

7 The seventh, to be regenerate, as *Henochius* the King of the inferiour world.

These seven secrets a man of an honest and constant minde may learn of the Spirits, without any offence unto God.

The mean Secrets are likewise seven in number.

1. The first is, the transmutation of Metals, which is vulgarly called *Alchymy*; which certainly is given to very few, and not but of special grace.

2. The second is, the curing of diseases with Metals, either by the magnetick vertues of precious stones, or by the use of the Philosophers stone, and the like.

3 The third is, to be able to perform Astronomical and Mathematical miracles, such as are *Hydraulick*-engines, to

administer business by the influence of Heaven, and things which are of the like sort.

4. The fourth is, to perform the works of natural Magick, of what sort soever they be.

5. The fifth is, to know all Physical secrets.

6. The sixth is, to know the foundation of all Arts which are exercised with the hands and offices of the body.

7. The seventh is, to know the foundation of all Arts which are exercised by the angelical nature of man.

The lesser secrets are seven.

1. The first is, to do a thing diligently, and to gather together much money.

2. The second is, to ascend from a mean state to dignities and honours, and to establish a newer family, which may be illustrious and do great things.

3. The third is, to excel in military affairs, and happily to achieve to great things, and to be an head of the head of Kings and Princes.

4. To be a good house-keeper both in the Country and City.

5. The fifth is, to be an industrious and fortunate Merchant.

6. To be a Philosopher, Mathematician, and Physician, according to *Aristotle, Plato, Ptolomy, Euclides, Hippocrates,* and *Galen.*

7. To be a Divine according to the Bible and Schooles, which all writers of divinity both old and new have taught.

Aphor. 25.

We have already declared what a secret is, the kindes and species thereof: it remaineth now to shew how we may attain to know those things which we desire.

The true and onely way to all secrets, is to have recourse unto God the Author of all good; and as Christ teacheth, *In the first place seek ye the kingdom of God and his righteousness, and all these things shall be added unto you.*

2. Also see that your hearts be not burthened with surfeting, and drunkenness, and the cares of this life.

3. Also commit your cares unto the Lord, and he will do it.

4. Also I the Lord thy God do teach thee, what things are profitable for thee, and do guide thee in the way wherein thou walkest.

5. And I will give thee understanding, and will teach thee in the way wherein thou shalt go, and I will guide thee with my eye.

6 Also if you which are evil, know how to give good things to your children, how much more shall your Father which is in heaven give his holy Spirit to them that ask him?

7. If you will do the will of my Father which is in heaven, ye are truly my disciples, and we will come unto you, and make our abode with you.

If you draw these seven places of Scripture from the letter unto the Spirit, or into action, thou canst out erre, but shalt attain to the desired bound; thou shalt not erre from the mark, and God himself by his holy Spirit will teach thee true and profitable things: he will give also his ministring Angels unto thee, to be thy companions, helpers, and teachers of all the secrets of the world, and he will command every creature to be obedient unto thee, so that cheerfully rejoycing thou maist say with the Apostles, That the Spirits are obedient unto thee; so that at length thou shalt be certain of the greatest thing of all, That thy name is written in Heaven.

Aphor. 26.

There is another way which is more common, that secrets may be revealed unto thee also, when thou art unwitting thereof, either by God, or by Spirits which have secrets in their power; or by dreams, or by strong imaginations and impressions, or by the constellation of a nativity by celestial knowledge. After this manner are made heroick men, such as there are very many, and all learned men in the world, *Plato, Aristotle, Hippocrates, Galen, Euclides, Archimedes, Hermes Trismegistus* the father secrets, with *Theophrastus, Paracelsus*; all which men had in themselves all the vertues of secrets. Hitherto also are referred, *Homer, Hesiod, Orpheus, Pytagoras*; but these had not such gifts of secrets as the former. To this are referred, the Nymphes, and sons of *Melusina*, and Gods of the Gentiles, *Achilles, Æneas, Hercules*: also, *Cyrus, Alexander* the great, *Julius Cæsar, Lucullus, Sylla. Marius.*

It is a canon, That every one know his own Angel. and that he obey him according to the word of God; and let him beware of the snares of the evil Angel, lest he be involved in the calamities of *Brute* and *Marcus Antonius.* To this refer the book of *Jovianus Pontanus* of Fortune, and his *Eutichus.*

The third way is, diligent and hard labor, without which no great thing can be obtained from the divine Deity worthy admiration, as it is said,

Tu nihil invita dices facie sue Minerva.

Nothing canst thou do or say against *Minerva*'s will.

We do detest all evil Magicians, who make themselves associates with the devils with their unlawful superstitions, and do obtain and effect some things which God permitteth to be done, instead of the punishment of the devils. So also they do other evil acts, the devil being the author, as the Scripture testifie of *Judas.* To these are referred all idolaters of old, and of our age, and abusers of Fortune, such as the heathens are full of. And to these do appertain all Charontick evocation of Spirits the works of *Saul* with the woman, and *Lucanus* prophesie of the deceased souldier, concerning the event of the Pharsalian war, and the like.

Make a Circle with a center A, which is B. C. D. E. At the East let there be B.C. a square. At the North, C.D. At the West, D.E. And at the South, E.D. Divide the Several quadrants into seven parts, that there may be in the whole 28 parts: and let them be again divided into four parts, that there may be 112 parts of the Circle: and so many are the true secrets to revealed. And this Circle in this manner divided, is the seal of the secrets of the world, which they draw from the onely center A, that is, from the invisible God, unto the whole creature. The Prince of the Oriental secrets is resident in the middle, and hath three Nobles on either side, every one whereof hath four under him, and the Prince himself hath four appertaining unto him. And in this manner the other Princes and Nobles have their quadrants of secrets, with their four secrets. But the Oriental secret is the study of all wisdom; The West, of strength; The South, of tillage; The North, of more rigid life. So that the Eastern secrets are commended to be the best; the Meridian to be mean; and the East and North to be lesser. The use of this seal of secrets is, that thereby thou maist know whence the Spirits or Angels are produced, which may teach the secrets delivered unto them from God. But they have names taken from their offices and powers, according to the gift which God hath severally distributed to every one of them. One hath the power of the sword; another, of the pestilence; and another, of inflicting famine upon the people, as it is ordained by God. Some are destroyers of Cities, as those two were, who were sent to overthrow *Sodom* and *Gomorrha*, and the places adjacent, examples whereof the holy Scripture witnesseth. Some are the watch-men over Kingdoms; others the keepers of private persons; and from thence, anyone may easily form their names in his own language: so that he which will, may ask a physical Angel, mathematical, or philosophical, or an Angel of civil wisdom, or of supernatural or natural wisdom, or for any thing whatsoever; and let him ask seriously, with a great desire of his minde, and with faith and constancy and without doubt, that which he asketh he shall receive from the Father and God of all Spirits. This faith surmounteth all seals, and bringeth them into subjection to the will of man. The Characteristical maner of calling Angels succeedeth this faith, which dependeth onely on divine revelation; But without the said faith preceding it, it lieth in obscurity. Nevertheless, if any one will use them for a memorial, and not otherwise, and as a thing simply created by God to his purpose, to which such a spiritual power or essence is bound; he may use them without any offence unto God. But let him beware, lest that he fall into idolatry, and the snares of the devil, who with his cunning sorceries, easily deceiveth the unwary. And he is not taken but onely by the finger of God, and is appointed to the service of man; so that they unwillingly serve the godly; but not without temptations and tribulations, because the commandment hath it, That he shall bruise the heel of Christ, the seed of the woman. We are therefore to exercise our selves about spiritual things, with fear and trembling, and with great reverence towards God, and to be conversant in spiritual essences with gravity and justice. And he which medleth with such things, let him beware of all levity, pride, covetousness, vanity, envy and ungodliness, unless he wil miserably perish.

Aphor. 28.

Because all good is from God, who is onely good, those things which we would obtain of him, we ought to seek them by prayer in Spirit and Truth, and a simple heart. The conclusion of the secret of secrets is, That every one exercise himself in prayer, for those things which he desires, and he shall not suffer a repulse. Let not any one despise prayer; for by whom God is prayed unto, to him he both can and will give. Now let us acknowledge him the Author, from whom let us humbly seek for our desires. A merciful & good Father, loveth the sons of desires, as *Daniel*; and sooner heareth us, then we are able to overcome the hardness of our hearts to pray. But he will not that we give holy things to dogs, nor despise and condemn the gifts of his treasury. Therefore diligently and often read over and over the first Septenary of secrets, and guide and direct thy life and all thy thoughts according to those precepts; and all things shall yield to the desires of thy minde in the Lord, to whom thou trustest.

The Fifth Septenary

Aphor. 29.

As our study of Magick proceedeth in order from general Rules premised, let us now come to a particular explication thereof. Spirits either are divine ministers of the word, and of the Church, and the members thereof ; or else they are servient to the Creatures in corporal things, partly for the salvation of the soul and body, and partly for its destruction. And there is nothing done, whether good or evil, without a certain and determinate order and government. He that seeketh after a good end, let him follow it; and he that desires an evil end, pursueth that also, and that earnestly, from divine punishment, and turning away from the divine will. Therefore let every one compare his ends with the word of God, and as a touchstone that will judge between good and evil; and let him propose unto himself what is to be avoided, and what is to be sought after; and that which he constituteth and determineth unto himself, let him diligently, not procrastinating or delaying, until he attain to his appointed bound.

Aphor. 30.

They which desire riches, glory of this world, Magistracy, honours, dignities, tyrannies, (and that magically) if they endeavour diligently after them, they shall obtain them, every one according to his destiny, industry, and magical Sciences, as the History of *Melesina* witnesseth, and the Magicians thereof, who ordained, That none of the Italian nation should for ever obtain the Rule or Kingdom of Naples; and brought it to pass, that he who reigned in his age, to be thrown down from his seat: so great is the power of the guardian or tutelar Angels of Kingdoms of the world.

Aphor. 31.

Call the Prince of the Kingdom, and lay a command upon him, and command what thou wilt, and it shall be done, if that Prince be not again absolved from his obedience by a succeeding Magician. Therefore the Kingdom of *Naples* may be again restored to the Italians, if any Magician shall call him who instituted this order, and compel him to recal his deed; he may be compelled also, to restore the secret powers taken from the treasury of Magick; A Book, a Gemme, and magical Horn, which being had, any one may easily, if he will, make himself the Monarch of the world. But *Judæus* chused rather to live among

Gods, until the judgement, before the transitory good of this world; and his heart is so blinde, that he understandeth nothing of the God of heaven and earth, or thinketh more, but enjoyeth the delights of things immortal, to his own eternal destruction. And he may be easier called up, then the Angel of *Plotinus* in the Temple of *Isis*.

Aphor. 32.

In like manner also, the Romans were taught by the Sibyls books; and by that means made themselves the Lords of the world, as Histories witness. But the Lords of the Prince of a Kingdom do bestow the lesser Magistracies. He therefore that desireth to have a lesser office, or dignity, let him magically call a Noble of the Prince, and his desire shall be fulfilled.

Aphor. 33.

But he who coveteth contemptible dignities, as riches alone, let him call the Prince of riches, or one of his Lords, and he shall obtain his desire in that kinde, whereby he would grow rich, either in earthly goods, or merchandize, or with the gifts of Princes, or by the study of Metals, or Chymistry: as he produceth any president of growing rich by these means, he shall obtain his desire therein.

Aphor. 34.

All manner of evocation is of the same kinde and form, and this way was familiar of old time to the Sibyls and chief Priests. This in our time, through ignorance and impiety, is totally lost; and that which remaineth, is depraved with infinite lyes and superstitions.

Aphor. 35.

The humane understanding is the onely effecter of all wonderful works, so that it be joyned to any Spirit; and being joyned, she produceth what she will. Therefore we are carefully to proceed in Magick, lest that Syrens and other monsters deceive us, which likewise do desire the society of the humane soul. Let the Magician carefully hide himself alwaies under the wings of the most High, lest he offer himself to be devoured of the roaring Lion; for they who desire earthly things, do very hardly escape the snares of the devil.

The sixth Septenary.

Care is to be taken, that experiments be not mixed with experiments; but that every one be onely simple and several: for God and Nature have ordained all things to a certain and appointed end: so that for examples sake, they who perform cures with the most simple herbs and roots, do cure the most happily of all. And in this manner, in Constellations, Words and Characters, Stones, and such like, do lie hid the greatest influences or vertues in deed, which are in stead of a miracle.

So also are words, which being pronounced, do forthwith cause creatures both visible and invisible to yield obedience, aswel creatures of this our world, as of the watry, aëry, subterranean, and Olympick supercelestial and infernal, and also the divine.

Therefore simplicity is chiefly to be studied, and the knowledge of such simples is to be sought for from God; otherwise by no other means or experience they can be found out.

And let all lots have their place decently: Order, Reason and Means, are the three things which do easily render all learning aswell of the visible as invisible creatures. This is the course of Order, That some creatures are creatures of the light; others, of darkness: these are subject to vanity, because they run headlong into darkness, and inthral themselves in eternal punishments for their rebellion. Their Kingdom is partly very beautiful in transitory and corruptible things on the one part, because it cannot consist without some vertue and great gifts of God; and partly most filthy and horrid to be spoken of, because it aboundeth with all wickedness and sin, idolatry, contempt of God, blasphemies against the true God and his works, worshippers of devils, disobedience towards Magistrates, seditions, homicides, robberies, tyranny, adulteries, wicked lusts, rapes, thefts, lyes, perjuries, pride, and a covetous desire of rule; in this mixture consisteth the kingdom of darkness: but the creatures of the light are filled with eternal truth, and with the grace of God, and are Lords of the whole world, and do reign over the Lords of darkness, as the members of Christ. Between these and the other, there is a continual war, until God shall put an end to their strife, by his last judgement.

Aphor. 38.

Therefore Magick is twofold in its first division; the one is of God, which he bestoweth on the creatures of light; the other also is of God, but as it is the gift which he giveth unto the creatures of darkness: and this is also two-fold: the one is to a good end, as when the Princes of darkness are compelled to do good unto the creatures, God enforcing them; the other is for an evil end, when God permitteth such to punish evil persons, that magically they are deceived to destruction; or, also he commandeth such to be cast out into destruction.

The second division of Magick is, that it bringeth to pass some works with visible instruments, through visible things; and it effecteth other works with invisible instruments by invisible things; and it acteth other things, aswel with mixed means, as instruments and effects.

The third division is, There are some things which are brought to pass by invocation of God alone: this is partly Prophetical, and Philosophical; and partly, as it were Theophrastical.

Other things there are, which by reason of the ignorance of the true God, are done with the Princes of Spirits, that his desires may be fulfilled; such is the work of the Mercurialists.

The fourth division is, That some exercise their Magick with the good Angels in stead of God, as it were descending down from the most high God: such was the Magick of *Baalim.*

Another Magick is, that which exerciseth their actions with the chief of the evil Spirits; such were they who wrought by the minor Gods of the heathens.

The fifth division is, That some do act with Spirits openly, and face to face; which is given to few: others do work by dreams and other signs; which the ancients took from their auguries and sacrifices.

The sixth division is, That some work by immortal creatures, others by mortal Creatures, as Nymphs, Satyrs, and such-like inhabitants of other elements, Pigmies, &c.

The seventh division is, That the Spirits do serve some of their own accord, without art; others they will scarce attend, being called by art.

Among these species of Magick, that is the most excellent of all, which dependeth upon God alone. The second, Them whom the Spirits do serve faithfully of their own accord. The third is, that

which is the property of Christians, which dependeth on the power of Christ which he hath in heaven and earth.

Aphor. 39.

There is a seven-fold preparation to learn the Magick Art.

The first is, to meditate day and night how to attain to the true knowledge of God, both by his word revealed from the foundation of the world; as also by the seal of the creation, and of the creatures; and by the wonderful effects which the visible and invisible creatures of God do shew forth.

Secondly it is requisite, that a man descend down into himself, and chiefly study to know himself; what mortal part he hath in him, and what immortal; and what part is proper to himself, and what diverse.

Thirdly, That he learn by the immortal part of himself, to worship, love and fear the eternal God, and to adore him in Spirit and Truth; and with his mortal part, to do those things which he knoweth to be acceptable to God, and profitable to his neighhours.

These are the three first and chiefest precepts of Magick, wherewith let every one prepare himself that covets to obtain true Magick or divine wisdom, that he may be accounted worthy thereof, and one to whom the Angelical creatures willingly do service, not occultly onely, but also manifestly, and as it were face to face.

Fourthly, Whereas every man is to be vigilant to see to what kinde life he shall be called from his mothers wombe, that every one may know whether he be born to Magick, and to what species thereof, which every one may perceive easily that readeth these things, and by experience may have success therein; for such things and such gifts are not given but onely to the low and humble.

In the fifth place we are to take care, that we understand when the Spirits are assisting us, in undertaking the greatest business; and he that understands this, it is manifest, that he shall be made a Magician of the ordination of God; that is, such a person who useth the ministery of the Spirits to bring excellent things to pass. Here, as for the most part, they sin, either through negligence, ignorance, or contempt, or by too much superstition; they offend also by ingratitude towards God, whereby many famous men have afterwards drawn upon themselves destruction: they sin also by rashness and obstinacy; and also when they do not use their

gifts for that honor of God which is required, and do prefer
πέριοχα ἐριρις.

Sixthly, The Magitian [sic] hath need of faith and taciturnity, especially, that he disclose no secret which the Spirit hath forbid him, as he commanded *Daniel* to seal some things, that is, not to declare them in publick; so as it was not lawful for *Paul* to speak openly of all things which he saw in a vision. No man will believe how much is contained in this one precept.

Seventhly, In him that would be a Magician, there is required the greatest justice, that he undertake nothing that is ungodly, wicked or unjust, nor to let it once come in his minde; and so he shall be divinely defended from all evil.

Aphor. 40.

When the Magician determineth with himself to do any incorporeal thing either with any exteriour or interiour sense, then let him govern himself according to these seven subsequent laws, to accomplish his Magical end.

The first Law is this, That he know that such a Spirit is ordained unto him from God; and let him meditate that God is the beholder of all his thoughts and actions; therefore let him direct all the course of his life according to the rule prescribed in the word of God.

Secondly, Alwaies pray with *David, Take not thy holy Spirit from me; and strengthen me with thy free Spirit; and lead us not into temptation, but deliver us from evil: I beseech thee, O heavenly Father, do not give power to any lying Spirit, as thou didst over* Ahab *that he perished; but keep me in thy truth.* Amen.

Thirdly, Let him accustome himself to try the Spirits, as the Scripture admonisheth; for grapes cannot be gathered of thorns: let us try all things, and hold fast that which is good and laudable, that we may avoid every thing that is repugnant to the divine power.

The fourth is, To be remote and cleer from all manner of superstition; for this is superstition, to attribute divinity in this place to things, wherein there is nothing at all divine; or to chuse or frame to our selves, to worship God with some kinde of worship which he hath not commanded: such are the Magical ceremonies of Satan, whereby he impudently offereth himself to be worshipped as God.

The fifth thing to be eschewed, is all worship of Idols, which bindeth any divine power to idols or other things of their own proper motion, where they are not placed by the Creator, or by the order of Nature: which things many false and wicked Magitians faign.

Sixthly, All the deceitful imitations and affections of the devil are also to be avoided, whereby he imitateth the power of the creation, and of the Creator, that he may so produce things with a word, that they may not be what they are. Which belongeth onely to the Omnipotency of God, and is not communicable to the creature.

Seventhly, Let us cleave fast to the gifts of God, and of his holy Spirit, that we may know them, and diligently embrace them with our whole heart, and all our strength.

Aphor. 41.

We come now to the nine last Aphorismes of this whole Tome; wherewith we will, the divine mercy assisting us, conclude this whole Magical *Isagoge*.

Therefore in the first place it is to be observed, what we understand by Magitian in this work.

Him then we count to be a Magitian, to whom by the grace of God. the spiritual essences do serve to manifest the knowledge of the whole universe, & of the secrets of Nature contained therein, whether they are visible or invisible. This description of a Magitian plainly appeareth, and is universal.

An evil Magician is he, whom by the divine permission the evil Spirits do serve, to his temporal and eternal destruction and perdition to deceive men, and draw them away from God; such was *Simon Magus*, of whom mention is made in the *Acts of the Apostles*, and in *Clemens;* whom Saint *Peter* commanded to be thrown down upon the earth, when as he had commanded himself, as it were a God, to be raised up into the air by the unclean Spirits.

Unto this order are also to be referred all those who are noted in the two Tables of the Law; and are set forth with their evil deeds.

The subdivisions and species of both kindes of Magick, we will note in the Tomes following. In this place it shall suffice, that we distinguish the Sciences, which is good, and which is evil:

Whereas man sought to obtain them both at first, to his own ruine and destruction, as *Moses* and *Hermes* do demonstrate.

Aphor. 42.

Secondly, we are to know, That a Magitian is a person predestinated to this work from his mothers wombe; neither let him assume any such great things to himself, unless he be called divinely by grace hereunto, for some good end; to a bad end is, that the Scripture might be fulfilled, *It must be that offences will come; but wo be to that man through whom they come.* Therefore, as we have before oftentimes admonished, With fear and trembling we must live in this world.

Notwithstanding I will not deny, but that some men may with study and diligence obtain some species of both kindes of Magick if it may be admitted. But he shall never aspire to the highest kindes thereof; yet if he covet to assail them, he shall doubtless offend both in soul and body. Such are they, who by the operations of false Magicians, are sometimes carried to Mount *Horch,* or in some wilderness, or desarts [deserts]; or they are maimed in some member, or are simply torn in pieces, or are deprived of their understanding; even as many such things happen by the use thereof, where men are forsaken by God, and delivered to the power of Satan.

The Seventh Septenary.

The Lord liveth, and the works of God do live in him by his appointment whereby he willeth them to be; for he will have them to use their liberty in obedience to his commands, or disobedience thereof. To the obedient, he hath proposed their rewards; to the disobedient he hath propounded their deserved punishment. Therefore these Spirits of their freewil, through their pride and contempt of the Son of God, have revolted from God their Creator, and are reserved unto the day of wrath; and there is left in them a very great power in the creation; but notwithstanding it is limited, and they are confined to their bounds with the bridle of God. Therefore the Magitian of God, which signifies a wise man of God, or one informed of God, is led forth by the hand of God unto all everlasting good, both mean things, and also the chiefest corporal things.

Great is the power of Satan, by reason of the great sins of men. Therefore also the Magitians of Satan do perform great things, and greater then any man would believe: although they do subsist in their own limits, nevertheless they are above all humane apprehension, as to the corporal and transitory things of this life; which many ancient Histories, and daily Examples do testitie. Both kindes of Magick are different one from the other in their ends: the one leadeth to eternal good, and useth temporal things with thanksgiving; the other is a little sollicitous about eternal things; but wholly exerciseth himself about corporal things, that he may freely enjoy all his lusts and delights in contempt of God and his anger.

Aphor. 44.

The passage from the common life of man unto a Magical life, is no other but a sleep, from that life; and an awaking to this life; for those things which happen to ignorant and unwise men in their common life, the same things happen to the willing and knowing Magitian.

The Magitian understandeth when the minde doth meditate of himself; he deliberateth, reasoneth, constituteth and determineth what is to be done; he observeth when his cogititions do proceed from a divine separate essence, and he proveth of what order that divine separate essence is.

But the man that is ignorant of Magick, is carried to and fro, as it were in war with his affections; he knoweth not when they issue out of his own minde, or are impressed by the assisting essence; and he knoweth not how to overthrow the counsels of his enemies by the word of God, or to keep himself from the snares and deceits of the tempter.

Aphor. 45.

The greatest precept of Magic is, to know what every man ought to receive for his use from the assisting Spirit, and what to refuse: which he may learn of the Psalmist, saying, *Wherewith shall a yong man cleanse his way? in keeping thy word, Oh Lord.* To keep the word of God, so that the evil one snatch it not out of the heart, is the chiefest precept of wisdom. It is lawful to admit of, and exercise other suggestions which are not contrary to the glory of God, and charity towards our neighbours, not inquiring from what Spirit such suggestions proceed: But we ought to take heed, that we are not too much busied with unnecessary things according to the admonition of Christ; *Martha, Martha, thou art troubled about many things; but Mary hath chosen the better part, which shall not be taken from her.* Therefore let us alwaies have regard unto the saying of Christ, *Seek ye first the kingdom of God and his righteousness, and all these things shall be added unto you.* All other things, that is, all things which are due to the mortal Microcosme, as food, raiment, and the necessary arts of this life.

Aphor. 46.

There is nothing so much becometh a man, as constancy in his words and deeds, and when the like rejoyceth in his like; there are none more happy then such, because the holy Angels are conversant about such, and possess the custody of them: on the contrary, men that are unconstant are lighter then nothing, and rotten leaves. We chuse the 46 Aphorisme from these. Even as every one governeth himself, so he allureth unto himself Spirits of his nature and condition; but one very truely adviseth, that no man should carry himself beyond his own calling, lest that he draw unto himself some malignant Spirit from the uttermost parts of the earth, by whom either he shall be infatuated and deceived, or brought to final destruction. This precept appeareth most plainly: for *Midas*, when he would convert all things into gold, drew up such a Spirit unto himself, which was able to perform this; and being deceived by him, he had been brought to death by famine, if his foolishness had not been corrected by the mercy of God. The same thing happened to a certain woman about *Franckford* at *Odera*, in our times, who would scrape together & devour mony of any thing. Would that men would diligently weigh this precept, and not account the Histories of *Midas,* and the like, for fables; they would be much more diligent in moderating their thoughts and affections, neither would they be so perpetually vexed with the Spirits of the golden mountains of

Utopia. Therefore we ought most diligently to observe, that such presumptions should be cast out of the minde, by the word, while they are new; neither let them have any habit in the idle minde, that is empty of the divine word.

Aphor. 47.

He that is faithfully conversant in his vocation, shall have also the Spirits constant companions of his desires, who will successively supply him in all things. But if he have any knowledge in Magick, they will not be unwilling to shew him, and familiarly to converse with him, and to serve him in those several ministeries, unto which they are addicted; the good Spirits in good things, unto salvation; the evil Spirits in every evil thing, to destruction. Examples are not wanting in the Histories of the whole World; and do daily happen in the world. *Theodosius* before the victory of *Arbogastus*, is an example of the good; *Brute* before he was slain, was an example of the evil Spirits, when he was persecuted of the Spirit of *Cæsar*, and exposed to punishment, that he slew himself, who had slain his own Father, and the Father of his Country.

Aphor. 48.

All Magick is a revelation of Spirits of that kinde, of which sort
the Magick is; so that the nine Muses are called, in *Hesiod*, the
ninth Magick, as he manifestly testifies of himself in *Theogony*. In
Homer, the genius of *Ulysses* in *Psigiogagia*. *Hermes*, the Spirits of the
more sublime parts of the minde. God revealed himself to *Moses*
in the bush. The three wise men who came to seek Christ at
Jerusalem, the Angel of the Lord was their leader. The Angels of
the Lord directed *Daniel*. Therefore there is nothing whereof any
one may glory; *For it is not unto him that willeth, nor unto him that
runneth; but to whom God will have mercy,* or of some other spiritual
fate. From hence springeth all Magick, and thither again it will
revolve, whether it be good or evil. In this manner *Tages* the first
teacher of the Magick of the Romanes, gushed out of the earth.
Diana of the Ephesians shewed her worship, as if it had been sent
from heaven. So also *Apollo*. And all the Religion of the Heathens
is taken from the same Spirits; neither are the opinions of the
Sadduces, humane inventions.

Aphor. 49.

The conclusion therefore of this *Isagoge* is the same which we have
above already spoken of, That even as there is one God, from
whence is all good; and one sin, to wit, disobedience, against the

will of the commanding God, from whence comes all evil; so that *the fear of God is the beginning of all wisdom,* and the profit of all Magick; for obedience to the will of God, followeth the fear of God; and after this, do follow the presence of God and of the holy Spirit, and the ministery of the holy Angels, and all good things out of the inexhaustible treasures of God.

But unprofitable and damnable Magick ariseth from this; where we lose the fear of God out of our hearts, and suffer sin to reign in us, there the Prince of this world, the God of this world beginneth, and setteth up his kingdom in stead of holy things, in such as he findeth profitable for his kingdom; there, even as the spider taketh the flye which falleth into his web, so Satan spreadeth abroad his nets, and taketh men with the snares of covetousness, until he sucketh him, and draweth him to eternal fire: these he cherisheth and advanceth on high, that their fall may be the greater.

Courteous Reader, apply thy eyes and minde to the sacred and profane Histories, & to those things which thou seest daily to be done in the world, and thou shalt finde all things full of Magick, according to a two-fold Science, good and evil, which that they may be the better discerned, we will put here their division and subdivision, for the conclusion of these *Isagoges*; wherein every one may contemplate, what is to be followed, and which to be avoided, and how far it is to be labored for by every one, to a competent end of life and living.

	Theoso-phy	• Knowledge of the Word of God, and ruling ones life according to the word of God. • Knowledge of the government of God by Angels, which the Scripture calleth watchmen; and to understand the mystery of Angels.
Good	Anthro-sophy given to man	• Knowledge of natural things. • Wisdom in humane things.
Sciences		
	Cakosi-phy	• Contempt of the word of God, and to live after the will of the devil. • Ignorance of the government of God by Angels • To contemne the custody of the Angels, and that their companions are of the devil. • Idolatry. • Atheisme.
Evil		
	Cacoc.mony	• The knowledge of poisons in nature, and to use them. • Wisdom in all evil arts, to the destruction of mankinde, and to use them in contempt of God, and for the loss and destruction of men.

FINIS.

(End of the Arbatel of Magick integral text)

Arbatel correspondence chart

The more you bring together correspondences in your ritual, the more powerful it will be. Still, the more virtuous you become, the more efficient the operations will be, and the more tangible the manifestations. You could have no correspondence to any other attribute but the specific virtue in your heart and mind, and the operation would be more efficient than if you had all the correspondences without the acquired virtue. Nonetheless, by developing yourself, mind and heart, and joining together as much correspondence as possible, you will get the most powerful results.

• Do the ritual on the suggested day
• Engrave the symbol at the base of a candle of the according color
• Have a number of candles according to the correspondence
• Invoke the name of the Spirit a corresponding number of times
• Pray God whit his name for the specific manifestation
• Invoke in the name of the corresponding archangel
• Do deep and long powerful breaths a certain number of times
• Visualize the accurate symbol, with willpower
• Speak high and loud, with determination
• Develop your spiritual virtues
• Face the suggested direction

Spirit	**Phul**	**Phaleg**	**Ophiel**	**Bethor**
Department	Life, energy, sensibility, fecundity.	Strength, war, apply justice, health.	Knowledge, psychic abilities, understanding.	Peace, define justice, authority.
Name of God	Shadaï El-Haï	Elohim Gibor	Elohim Tzebaoth	EL
Archangel	Gabriel	Kamael	Raphael	Tzadkiel
Day	Monday	Tuesday	Wednesday	Thursday
Color, primary and secondary	Violet and blue	Red	Orange and yellow	Blue and violet
Number	9	5	8	4
Direction	West	South	East	East
Virtue	Hope	Strength	Prudence	Justice
Sin to vanquish	Avarice	Anger	Laziness	Envy

Spirit	**Hagith**	**Aratron**	**Och**
Department	Love, creativity, sensuality, sexuality.	Death, lessons of life, religion, transformation.	Success, power, abundance, health.
Name of God	Yod-He-Vav-He Tzebaoth	Yod-He-Vav-He	Eloha Ve-Daath
Archangel	Haniel	Tzaphkiel	Michael
Day	Friday	Saturday	Sunday
Color, primary and secondary	Green	Indigo and black	Gold/yellow and orange
Number	7	3	6
Direction	West	North	South
Virtue	Charity	Temperance	Faith
Sin to vanquish	Luxury	Gluttony	Pride

When you visualize the symbol, see it clearly in front of you, with a determined mind, willpower, self-trust, faith and integrity. See it glowing with the primary color, floating in an infinit environment of the secondary color. Do not push hard with your mind, like if you physically tried to raise your inner pressure. Relax yourself physically and practice developing your determination from within, at the emotional level with desire, at the willpower level with self-implication, and at the mental level with awareness and self-trust.

The direction of the operation is an extra correspondence that is not at all necessary, especially when it means you would have to move your entire altar setup if you have one. Those of you who do the ritual with a minimum installation can easily turn to the correct orientation, but this factor should not bother you. Has for the recommended day, it is also an amplification correspondence, but keep in mind that God is everything and the universe is alive at all times, and all the Olympic Spirits can be invoked whenever you wish.

Olympic symbols and names

The symbols always become more efficient when they are drawn as close as possible to the mathematical perfection they are based on. The symbols available in the translated text are accurate, but made by hand many hundred years ago. Here are the seven symbols of the Olympic Spirits redrawn with straight lines and accurate proportions.

The symbols are accompanied with a comment on the symbol, a concept to meditate upon when you master more of the science of kabbalah. The numeric value is very important to the kabbalists that make relations between words that have the same numeric value. They also use the tool of "gematria" by adding each digit to find the root number of the concept.

Each symbol can also be transposed on the Tree of Life to follow the concept of the flow of creative energy in the symbol. A lot of science was revealed thru the centuries, but I will not elaborate too much, so you can remain in the contemplative state while you establish your own communication with the Olympic Spirits.

Aratron

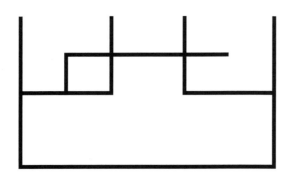

The left receptacle of Binah (intelligence) is linked from under with the right receptacle of Hochmah (wisdom-love). The two receptacles are seated on the spiritual structure Geburah-Hesed. And thru a direct link, the light from Binah flows back into the absolute subtle cosmic process, giving it's virtues to Aratron: transmutation, becoming invisible, funeral aspects... And as the flow returns to Binah, it is directly anchored to its receptacle, giving its other virtues: make the barren fruitful, ground properties, gives powers, extend life...

Aratron
Hebrew: (Aleph – Resh – Aleph – Thet – Resh – Vav – Noun)
It's numeric value (with a final Noun) is 1117. The gematria of 1117 is 10 (1 + 1 + 1 + 7 = 10), pointing out the relation to the earthly aspects of Malkuth (Kingdom). With 1 being the unity of the original consciousness, and seven being the concept of spiritual force, these four digits, associated to the four human planes will make:

1- Unity of mind,
1- Unity of emotion,
1- Unity of will,
7- Spiritual force manifested.

The advanced kabbalist will make the same relationship to the four levels of creation.

Bethor

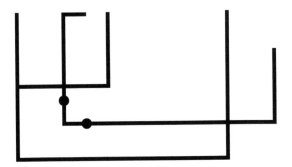

The left receptacle of Binah, seated again on the Geburah-Hesed structure, is pouring upwards, like a fountain, from Hesed (misericord) into Hochmah (wisdom-love). This movement is confirmed by a second link, taking the light directly into the receptacle of Binah, angled inwards like a buckler, and making the flow again into Hesed, and up towards Hochmah, like a sword. This is the result of the Justice aspects of Jupiter. The two links at the right raise Jupiter towards wisdom, standing for dignity, and they dissolve into wisdom, which makes the relation with the air aspect.

Bethor

Hebrew: (Beith – Thav – Vav – Resh)

It's value is 608. The gematria is 5 (6 + 0 + 8 = 14, 1 + 4 = 5), linking with the Justice and Strength of Geburah-Hesed.

Phaleg

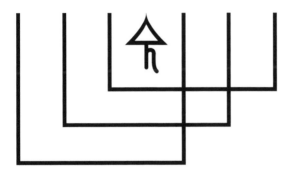

The symbol of Saturn mounted with a triangle indicates that the source is the higher trinity, passing thru Binah and pouring its force into Geburah (Strength). Geburah then acts in three ways, since the source was threefold, and will work on the cosmic, creative and formative levels.

Phaleg

Hebrew: (Phe – Lamed – Ghimel)

The value is 113, in relation with a stream (Peleg). The gematria is 5 (1 + 1 + 3 = 5) linking again with the Justice of Geburah-Hesed, and the force aspect of Geburah.

Och

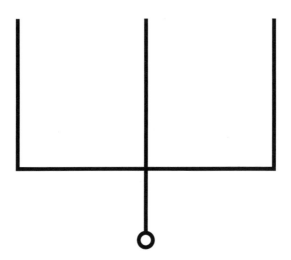

The Light of the three pillars pours down into the sun of Tiphereth. Binah and Hochmah are linked together, seated again on the Geburah-Hesed structure. Och receives it's virtues from the highest trinity, making royalty and all his solar properties.

Och

Hebrew: (Vav – Heth)

Its value is 14, the same value as the Hebrew word for "gold" (zahav), the metal of the sun, and the word for "hand" (yad), which is a symbol of power to rule. Again, a gematria of 5 (1 + 4 = 5), linking to the Geburah-Hesed structure.

Hagith

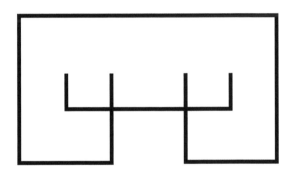

It is said that in the sephirah Netzah, all other sephiroth are found. The inner receptacle receives this Netzah, where everything is found. We can see that the Light pours down from Netzah, circles around all other spheres, and goes back into Netzah. The outer line encapsulates the creation, and the creation is symbolized by the four ends of each lines, attributed to the 4000 legions of Hagith. In another perspective, the symbol being placed over the Tree of Life, the receptacle appears right under

Tiphereth, receiving it's glorious light, while the outer line connect with Hod, Geburah, Hesed and Netzath, returning back to the inner receptacle.

Hagith

Hebrew: (He – Ghimel – Yod – Thav)

Its value is 418, the same value as the mysterious name of God « ABRAHADABRA », an important Kabbalah secret. It's gematria is 13 (4 + 1 + 8 = 13) the number of the Hebrew word for Love (ahavah), also the number of the Hebrew word for Unity (Achad), and 4 (1 + 3 = 4) referring to the important link of Hagith with the 4 elements of nature, and it's 4000 legions.

Ophiel

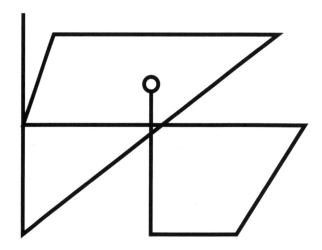

This symbol is the most complicated, and so does the link it holds with the sephirot trajectory. The little circle in the middle is the sun, placed at Tiphereth, so it starts with wisdom that enlightens. The flow goes down to the sephira Yesod to become more tangible, more accessible. It turns right, to go back up into the natural laws of Netzah, where it will become creative, then full left to Hod to become intellectually comprehensible. After what it elevates itself to the base of Geburah, grasping the strength of movement, and right to Hesed, to get the science of the powers. After contacting all of these sephoth, it strikes back down and left, to the base of the left pillar of rigor, to elevate the comprehension to the heavens, and finally end into contemplation of its movement.

Ophiel

Hebrew: (Aleph – Vav – Phe – Yod – Aleph – Lamed)

Its value is 128. Its gematria is 11 (1 + 2 + 8 = 11), being the first movements of consciousness into the cosmic motion. Not so clear, of course, simply contemplate to find out more.

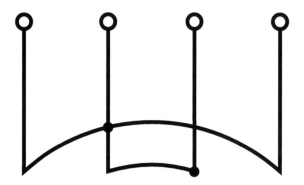

We can see the sun four times, one for each level of creation, shining down on the big arch of the moon, demonstrating the reflective aspects of the Light on the lower planes. The two suns at the extremes, linked down to the bigger moon crescent, refer to the highest level of the light shining down on the macrocosmic mirror of creation. The two inside suns shine down on the smaller moon mirror, which is closer (lower) to the human, being more accessible to us. It is the microcosmic reflection that we can contemplate to give us access to the higher consciousness, since they are inter-connected.

Phul
Hebrew: (Phe – Vav – Lamed)
Its value is 116, showing it's relation to the whirling energies (Galgalim = 116). Its gematria is 8 (1 + 1 + 6 = 8).

Elemental work

Elemental contact

There is a goal to contacting elemental spirits. If it would be only for fantasy and leisure, we would not even speak of their utility in this book. By being in contact with a being, you can experiment the traits of this being in yourself. We contact elemental spirits so that we can feel in our body, their virtues, their qualities, and even recognize their attributed flaw, so that we can become aware of our own flaws. We contact elemental spirits to grow with them.

Contrarily to other types of spirits, like angels, the elemental spirits do not obey to you because you did the ritual accordingly, with the good methods and formulas. They are attracted by the law of correspondence, like any other type of spirit, but they are also free, like humans. Their free-will obliges us to befriend them. They do not have to obey us, they only obey to their program, and they obey directly to a command of God. It would be pretentious of the human seeker to pretend being able to give them a command as God would do, and hope to be obeyed. This would only make them mad, and they would bestow a curse on you, not providing the help you requested. When a true occultist becomes illumed with his Divine Spirit, he may be recognized by the elementals as the incarnation of God. Until then, be humble and approach elemental spirits with gratitude and respect.

When in contact with an elemental spirit, you must let them see your heart, your true intentions, your real self. They will sense you, and provide their friendship at the level you have developed your virtues and qualities. To attract the friendship of a water elemental, you must be flexible in your decisions, and not subject to paranoia. To attract a wind elemental, you must be quick in your mind, and be honest. Each elemental spirit are attracted by a virtue and offended by a vice.

Once contacted, they can provide information of their elemental functions, and help you in your process of transformation. A more advanced ritualist can be more precise on his demands, but your must remember that any greedy request will result in offending the elemental spirit. With a good heart, you will succeed in asking just about anything, if you address yourself to the type of spirit who can accomplish the request.

In the next articles, you will learn each type of ritual to attract and befriend each type of elemental spirits. For now, here are the base aspects of your personality to work on, before you think about invoking an elemental spirit.

Earth elementals are attracted by perseverance and patience. They are offended by greed and haste.

Water elementals are attracted by flexibility, fluidity and imagination. They are offended by illusion, paranoia and erroneous fantasy.

Wind elementals are attracted by quickness, joy and honesty. They are offended by lies, disorder and sadness.

Fire elementals are attracted by power, movement, and determination. They are offended by anger, hatred and laziness. It is very highly recommended that you do not invoke a fire elemental until you are able to contain your anger in the most difficult situations.

Ritual of summoning

To summon an elemental spirit, you must have developed the virtue they are attracted to, and have worked on resolving the vice they are offended by. Do not wait until you are a perfect human being before you invoke them, but at least be aware and work on yourself. You can even ask the elemental spirit to help you develop a certain virtue, and get rid of a certain vice. You can ask help to heal your body, elevate your energy level, or develop a certain psychic ability...

The ritual must be in some place where you can find a lot of the element. For the earth elemental, go in a cave, or on a big mound of rocks, deep in nature. For the water elemental, go near a river, have containers of water all around you,... For wind elementals, go where there is a lot of wind, or have a lot of feathers with you. For the fire elemental, you should not try to go into a volcano, unless you have one in your backyard. Having a big fire would be enough, and lots of candles can also do the job if you are inside. Again, do not invoke a fire elemental unless you are a very mentally stable person, and do not get angry.

The items and names to invoke will be found on the following pages, treating each element separately. Get all of these items together, and set them in place, in a circle, in the good orientation, so that you can do the ritual for at least half an hour without being disturbed. Never interrupt a ritual of summoning. Make sure you will have peace. If you should be pressed to finish a ritual, at any time, put everything down, say "I thank you all for your presence, you should go now" and bow a bit. This is an emergency way out, like if someone comes into the room, or at the ritual site. Do not stop a ritual just to answer the phone or because you don't want to miss your favorite TV show.

Start by praying to God, using the Hebrew name associated by the art of Kabbalah. Ask God to bless your ritual, so that you can attain your goal. Then, invoke the archangel who is in charge of this elemental energy, by signing its name many times. Get into a meditative state, while keeping your eyes opened, and mentally focus on the element you are summoning. Along the ritual, you will let the elemental spirit reveal itself to you, in your mind, and maybe you will be able to see it on the ethereal plane, after a while of practice.

You will bow three times while saying "I bow to God (name of God), I bow to the archangel (name of Archangel), I bow to the kind (king of the element)".

Then, start burning some incense associated to the element. Draw its shape with the appropriate color, on a white paper. Draw around the shape the astrological signs associated. Draw inside the shape, the planetary symbols associated. Draw at the middle of the shape, the tetragrammic letter associated with it.

For a few minutes, meditate on the quality of the element, and visualize yourself surrounded by the colors of the element. If you can, keep in your hand a part of an animal associated with the element.

After a few deep breaths, invoke the name of the king of the element 3 times, and ask him to send you an elemental that serve him. Example: "Ghob, Ghob, Ghob, I invoke you, by the divine Adonaï ha-Aretz, by Uriel, here and now. I ask you to send me an earth elemental spirit, here and now, to manifest in front of me, around me, and thru me." Stay in a perceptive state. Keep your eyes opened, but keep your mind's eye aware as well.

Once a spirit approached you, either thru your mind or physically, salute it and ask for its name. Go on with your request, if any. It is suggested that the first times, you simply ask for its help on your spiritual path, and ask if there is anything he/she could tell you that will help you on your path. Have a little discussion if you wish, or you could chant a spiritual chant with the elemental spirit.

This could go on for a few minutes at first, but for an hour when experimented. Once you are done, thank the elemental for his presence. Remember it's name if you successfully heard it. You will use it to re-invoke the same elemental afterwards. Ask him to go, and that you will summon him at another time. Bow three times: thank the king of the element, thank the archangel for his assistance, and thank God for everything. Meditate for a while.

Of earth

Elementals: Gnomes

King: Ghob

God Name: Adonai ha-Aretz

Quadrical: North

Archangel: Uriel

Angel: Phorlakh

Angelic Order: Cherubim

Quality: Stability

Color: Yellow, brown, black, and rustic

Complementary Color: Blue

Tetragramic Letter: Second He

Form: Square, cross

Sense: Touch

Sign: Taurus

Magical tool: Pentagram

Focus: Senses

Created: Stones

Stones: Dark stones, and stones that help with grounding oneself

Metal: Lead, silver

Plants Anatomy: Roots

Animals: Burring animals

Musical Instrument: Drums

Musical Note: "f"

Planets: Moon, Saturn, and earth

Signs: Taurus, Virgo, and Capricorn's

Body: Feet to the knees, the body its self, bones

Finger: Thumb

Elemental creatures: Gnomes, brownies, elves, satyrs, pans, dryads, goblins, dwarfs, leprechauns, giants.

Herbs: Patchouli, mugwort, horehound, sagebrush, sorrel, vervain, magnolia, horsetail, salt, roots

Some Virtues: Patience, builder, strength, thrift, acquisition, conserved, practical, dependable, stable, endurance, protective

Some Vices: Greed, addictions, obsessions, laziness, tired, lack of control, forgetful, anger, slow

Phlegmatic Temperament: Respectable, endure, considerate, resolute, firm, serious, scrupulous, concentrative, sober, punctual, circumspective, resistant, dullness, tardiness, lazy, unreliable.

Of water

King: Nichsa

Elemental: Undines

God Name: Shaddai El Chai

Quadrical: West

Archangel: Gabriel

Angel: Taliahad

Angelic Order: Thrones, archangels

Quality: Contraction, magnetic

Color: White, blue

Complementary Color: Black

Tetragramic letter: First He

Form: Half moon

Sense: Taste

Sign: Scorpio

Magical Tool: Cup, crystal ball, mirrors

Focus: Emotions

Created: Metals

Stones: Pearl, crystals, and all stones associated with water, or of the color blue

Metal: Quicksilver, silver, yellow brass

Plant Anatomy: leaves

Animal: Fish

Musical instrument: String instruments

Musical note: "g"

Planet: Saturn, mercury, Moon, Neptune

Signs: Scorpio, cancer, Pisces

Body: Knees to waist, glands, sweat, and saliva

Finger: Ring finger

Elemental beings: Mermaids, ocenaid, nereides, limoniades, sprites, nixen, potamides, undines

Herbs: Aloe, apple, lemon balm, belladonna, birch, poplar, poppy, blackberry, burdock, camphor, chamomile, elder, ragwort, rose, coltsfoot, comfrey, daisy, daffodil, datura, sandalwood, yarrow, elm, eucalyptus, foxglove, hemlock, hemp, hibiscus, jasmine, yew, spearmint, thyme, kava-kava, ladies slipper, lemon, myrrh, morning glory, passion flower

Virtues: Receptive, understanding, empathic, sympathy, vitality, growth, loving, kind, astrally aware, divining, intune with cycles, meditative

Vices: Over emotional, disintegrating, dissolving, secretive, indifferent, no foundations, ungrounded, forgetful, lustful, clouded

Melancholic temperament: Respectful, modest, compassionate, devoted, serious, docile, fervour, cordiality, comprehensive, meditative, calm, quick, adaptable, forgiving, tender, indifferent, depressed, apathy, shyness, lazy

Of air

King: Paralda

Elementals: Sylphs

God Name: Elohim Tzaboath

Quadrical: East

Archangel: Michael

Angel: Chassan

Angelic Orders: Dominions, principalities

Quality: Reasoning

Color: Orange, yellow

Complimentary color: Violet

Tetragramic Letter: Vav

Form: Circle, dot

Sense: Smell, hearing

Sign: Aquarius

Magical Tools: Dagger, incense, and sword

Focus: Intellect

Created: Plants

Stones: Spongious, pumice stone, all stones with a yellowish tint

Metal: Copper, tin

Plants Anatomy: Flowers

Animals: Birds

Musical Instrument: Wind instruments

Musical Note: "e"

Planets: Jupiter, Venus, and Uranus

Signs: Aquarius, Libra, and Gemini

Body: Throat to forehead, ears, nose, skin, and all things with the respiratory system.

Finger: Little finger

Elemental Beings: Fays, fairies, sylphs, muses, dryads, pixies, hamadryads, chameleons

Herbs: Almond, aspen, benzoin, citron, clover, dandelion, eyebright, hazel, lavender, lemongrass, lily of the valley, mace, marjoram, mint, mistletoe, sage, savory, slippery elm, pine, parsley

Virtues: speed, communications, adaptability, magnetic, fluid, optimistic, clearness, kindness, intellectual, piercing, perceptive, inventive

Vices: Gossiper, thief, dishonest, contemptible, fearful, lacking of stability, rude, air headed, unemotional

The Four Winds:

Notus- south,cloudy, moist, and sickly

Boreas- north, fierce, roaring, frost

Zephyrus- west, soft, pleasant, cold, moist

Eurus- east, waterish, cloudy, ravenous

Sanguine Temperament: Penetrating, diligent, joy, Adroitness, dishonest, fickle, kind, clear, eager, contempt, Gossiper, lack of endurance

Of fire

King: Djin

Elemental: Salamanders

God Name: Yehovah Tzabaoth

Quadrical: South

Archangel: Raphael

Angel: Aral, Samuael

Angelic order: Seraphim, powers

Quality: Expansion, electric

Color: Red

Complimentary color: Green

Tetragramic letter: Yod

Form: Triangle

Sense: Sight

Sign: Leo

Magical Tool: Wand, candles, and some daggers

Focus: Will. understanding

Created: Animals

Stones: Asbestos, fire stones, or anything that is associated with fire or the color red

Metals: Gold, iron, steel, nickel, red brass

Plants anatomy: Seeds

Animals: Salamanders, crickets

Musical instrument: Voice

Musical note: "d"

Planets: Mars, sun, Pluto

Signs: Leo, Aries, and Sagittarius

Body: Waist to throat; eyes, blood, and nerves

Finger: Index finger

Elemental Beings: Acthnici, salamanders, dragons, crickets, drakes, basilisk, phoenix, sphinx

Herbs: Alder, ash, basil, blood root, cactus, cedar, cinnamon, copal, damiana, dragons blood, garlic, hawthorn, heliotrope, hyssop, juniper, mandrake, oak, onion, pepper, rue, st.johns wart, snapdragon, tobacco, wormwood, yucca, sulphur

Virtues: Energetic, strength, creative, valor, loyalty, motion, perceptive

Vices: Sporadic, breakative, irritable, destructive, intemperance, anger, caught in illusions

Choleric temperament: Activity, enthusiasm, eagerness, resolute, courage, productive, gluttony, jealous, passions, irritability, intemperance

Conclusion: Knight, priest and king

To be a knight is to master yourself and to act with virtue. It is a path of righteousness, justice and goodness. It is to be responsible for all your actions, to never blame the other for your flaws. It is to take care of your own heart with great Love, and to project this Love to others. Be compassionate with yourself and others. Never play the role of the victim, the savior or the persecutor. Be yourself, even if you do not know yourself. Practice, practice again. Look inside yourself for the truth, meditate, and let yourself live again as Spirit. Remember to smile and create happiness in your life.

To be a priest is to have faith in God and master the spiritual practices that enrich your contact with Him. It is the spiritual path undertaken with utmost adoration for all that is sacred, most of all, for the human heart. It is to be available to your fellow humans with the accurate discernment of what they really need from you. It is to keep the secrets of your occult discoveries for yourself, and to share the Happiness and the Joy of life with others. Speak of God only in the way others want to ear about. If need be, do not even mention the word "God". Never think you hold the truth. The truth is a state of mind, and not something you can posses. Do not force your vision on the mind of others, .

but enrich their own vision, hoping that they will discover God, in their own time, in their own way.

To be a king is to manage your human experience in perfect harmony with the Divine Truth. It is a path only for your self, not even to be suggested to others. It is to become Holy, a saint amongst the multitude. It is never again to believe in pain, but in experience. It is to guide your fellow humans out of misery, into happiness. It is to give a perfect example to others and to know that you can be a holy person in the eyes of God. A king seems to rule, but he is not a ruler; he is a servant to the people. It is the accomplishment of the seven seals in the human experience manifested outwardly only for the Glory of God.

Above all, seek Love, and the power will reveal itself to you. The path of virtue is the only path to take, in every occult system. All other tools are but accessories for the human ego to play with, while the Divine Spirit passes thru and redefines your human experience to reflect more of your Divine Self. To be a knight, a priest, and ultimately a king, all you have to do is seek Love; all you have to do is Love.

May God bless you and guide you on your path,

François Lépine

Made in the USA
Middletown, DE
20 May 2016